OTHER BOOKS BY KEN MANSFIELD

THE ROOF: The Beatle's Final Co̶n̶c̶e̶r̶t̶

HE WAS THERE! There were just a handful of people in the immediate area where the Beatles played as a live band for the last time. As former U.S. manager of Apple Records, Ken Mansfield offers a personal, entertaining, and historically accurate look at the Beatles' last concert while introducing readers to the inside stories and reflections of the Beatles and other characters in the vibrant decade of the sixties. All are interwoven with colorful descriptions on the workings, realities, and the true characters behind the cultural phenomenon that defined a generation. View the modern music industry from someone who was part of its growth and who lets you experience moments of music history that will never come again. **Ken Mansfield was there!**

> *"I lived through the record industry's most exciting years with Ken...it is a pleasure to experience so much of it all again through the accuracy of his story telling and the clarity of his memory."*
>
> **—Peter Asher, Peter and Gordon, A&R Chief of Apple Records, Multi Platinum producer**

PHILCO

Philco—a man whose name evokes the distant past—enters this world on the side of a desolate country road, having no idea who he is or why he is here. With only a satchel full of items holding clues to his identity, he travels to places both imaginary and real—following the answers that unfold along the way. Once Upon Another Time, There Was This Place, But You Can't Get There Anymore...From Here.

"If there was ever a ranking of 'Top 100 Most Interesting Lives in History,' Ken Mansfield would be on it. In Philco, he brings his experience and imagination to bear for you. This is a story that will stay with you forever."

—Andy Andrews, *New York Times* bestselling author of *The Traveler's Gift* and *The Noticer*

ROCK AND A HEART PLACE

A raw, sensitive, and unforgettable journey from sex, drugs, and rock and roll to sweet salvation. Ken takes readers on a mesmerizing journey alongside members of some of music's most iconic bands, including Kansas, Ozzy Osbourne, Korn, Prince, The Turtles, and The Byrds, just to name a few. Their recollections of the way things were offers a backstage pass into a bizarre world that in the end reveals the bigger picture of God's purpose for our lives.

"This fascinating and fun-to-read book is loaded with inside stories of some of our favorite music-makers. It is a classic reminder that regardless what messes our family or friends might encounter, the Creator is greater; nobody is beyond hope, and there is no need to give up on anyone!"

—Ken Abraham, *New York Times* bestselling author

STUMBLING ON OPEN GROUND

A story of trial and faith like those found in the books of Esther and Job. It's a private dialogue between Ken, his wife Connie, and the God who transformed them in the middle of a heartbreaking disease.

"Ken is jarringly honest about everything—life, success, fame, disillusionment, faith, cancer.... This

book might make you a little uncomfortable, but that's probably why you should read it."

—Bernie Leadon, founding member of The Eagles

BETWEEN WYOMINGS

Subtitled (My God and an iPod on the Open Road) is a modern-day Ecclesiastes tale, where with his wife, Connie, and a van named Moses, Ken metaphorically recreates the travels that took him into the homes and careers of entertainment legends. Readers are called to reflect on the highways of their own lives, the turns and detours that press them into the heart of a Creator who has been there all along.

"Mansfield's prayerful musings are quite extraordinary."

—Publishers Weekly

THE WHITE BOOK

An insider's view of an era that invites readers to know the characters of The Beatles and the musicians of their time— the bands that moved an industry and a culture to a whole new rhythm. This engaging and unusual account spans some of the most fertile and intense decades in music history.

"There is something quite Lennonesque about Ken Mansfield's soul searching—his tales are astonishingly clear and vivid."

—Barnes&Noble.com

To contact or order autographed books directly from Ken
MainMansfield.com

the BEATLES
the BIBLE
and BODEGA BAY

the BEATLES
the BIBLE
and BODEGA BAY

A LONG AND WINDING ROAD

Ken MANSFIELD

APPLE RECORDS FORMER U.S. MANAGER

Post Hill
PRESS

A POST HILL PRESS BOOK
ISBN: 978-1-63758-323-4
ISBN (eBook): 978-1-63758-324-1

The Beatles, The Bible and Bodega Bay:
A Long and Winding Road
© 2000 by Ken Mansfield
All Rights Reserved

Post Hill Press
New York • Nashville
posthillpress.com

Published in the United States of America
1 2 3 4 5 6 7 8 9 10

The Long and Winding Road

Past, present, and future abruptly blend into a rock and holy roll reflection in this uncanny presentation of outside facts and inside feelings by the author. As far apart as Bodega Bay, the Bible, and the Beatles would appear to be, Ken Mansfield draws them together via that intrinsic road map that dwells within the heart of every man and every woman.

Homerically, the journey itself is often the splendorous part of any destination. Ken's cryptic endeavor to assemble fragments of life's travels into some sense of eventual discovery, direction, and purpose of pilgrimage is the precious point of departure that force launches each reader back into their own personal time warps. There is no intent and no intensity in these revelations, only an intentional Vonneguttian bounce between events and musings. *The Beatles, The Bible and Bodega Bay* are parts and pieces that fit within the realm and range of either our imagined or empirically perceived realities. You are invited to absorb these offerings as you would a suntan. Afterward, you will probably look good in a white shirt or pale blue earrings.

Days in the Lives

Here, There, and Everywhere

THE BEATLES

In the history of twentieth-century popular music, no one has ever been, or possibly will ever be, as monumentally famous as Elvis Presley and the Beatles. The following pages offer a gentle, inside, and unique look at four of these five people as they traveled a musical bridge across the Atlantic Ocean into the hearts of their fans—and especially into the life of one young American record executive.

THE BIBLE

In the history of the printed word, no book has sold as many copies or lasted as long as this powerful collection of stories, observations, and parables. No other assemblage of authors' predictions and wisdom has ever proved as dependable or shaped the character of mankind as much as this inspired publication. Its words traveled an even longer distance across time into the heart of this same man.

BODEGA BAY

Historically famous as the home of Alfred Hitchcock's *The Birds* and one of northern California's last active fishing villages, Bodega Bay is a picturesque jewel-like town on the beautiful and turbulent Sonoma coast. While confusing to travelers, the siren attraction to those who dwell here is the enchanting juxtaposition of clapboard buildings, fine restaurants, rural attitudes, upscale art galleries, wine tastings by the sea, rugged fishermen, and exclusive country club homes that quietly share this scenic and sheltered harbor. It is to this place our time-torn traveler has taken his souvenirs and tattered baggage to unpack and put away.

Author's Bent, Intent, and Lament

As a record producer to many famous recording artists over the years, I have become used to product review and criticism. Therefore I will now take a different approach to this whole process and pre-answer the predictable criticism of the ramblings found bound between these covers.

To those who suggest that this is really two different books, I gently respond, "No it isn't." I can't write about recollections of the places I have been without the foundational realities of where I am now. If I had written this book twenty years ago, the chapters sandwiched between my Beatles remembrances would have probably been about drugs, rock concerts, and wild parties. My hard years in the music business are the reasons why I have now found a soft place out of the mainstream.

My nature has always been to live in the extremes. Nothing was more extreme than life in the fast lane of the entertainment world; nothing is more extremely beautiful than the peace I have now in my musings here on the edge of nowhere. The Beatles stories are mainly about my twenties and thirties, when my hormones were raging at an intensity matched only by my unbridled ambition. Now that the sun and the greater part of my daredevil determinations are simultaneously sinking slowly into the western horizon, I ask the reader to look at these times in a complete framework of what ultimately our lives are all about. If I had had any concept then about the whole picture, I would have probably planned things a little differently.

I hope everyone who reads this can find themselves somewhere in these chapters and will be surprised in the realization of how much there eventually is to each of us. The younger man in London—on top of the Apple building (and the world!) as he watches the Beatles perform for the last time—and the older man on a remote Sonoma beach—on his knees looking out to sea and into the heart of his Creator—are the same person. Yes, this is one story. It is written in the present, but it relives the call of the rock and roll world that still rings in my ears like a restless echo out of the past. It also reflects ahead to another roll call from the "Rock of Eternity"—eternity: the long part of our existence—that lives in my heart like a peaceful cool stream flowing into my future. Every man and every woman must have three elements to qualify for existence: a past, a present, and a future. If one of these is missing—then so are you!

For those who still insist that this is two different books, then consider *The Beatles, The Bible and Bodega Bay* as a "two for one" offer. If that doesn't work and the "other" stuff is of no interest, simply treat it like a hamburger—take the meat out and just eat the lettuce. Enjoy—and as John Lennon's mother once told him: "You've eaten the spuds, now give peas a chance."

A Foreword
from Back Then

Beatles & Co
3 Savile Row London W1
telephone 01-734 8232

31st July 1969.

Ken Mansfield Esq.,
Capitol Records Inc.,
1750 North Vine,
Hollywood and Vine,
Hollywood,
California 90028.
U.S.A.

Dear Ken,

Just a little note to congratulate you on your well
deserved promotion, which could not have gone to a
better man ... or a shorter one.

Thank you for looking after Apple Records.   Hope to
see you when you're here or I'm there.   Love to
Stan (Gortikov).

Yours, eventually,

FAMOUS
A Show-Bizz Personality
(Tricks on the High Wire a Speciality).

John Lennon Paul McCartney George Harrison Richard Starkey Apple Corps

Preludes

THE BEATLES

There are places I remember all my life
Though some have changed
Some forever not for better
Some have gone and some remain
All these places have their moments
With lovers and friends I still can recall
Some are dead and some arc living
In my life I loved them all

LENNON AND MCCARTNEY

THE BIBLE

The whole Bible was given to us by inspiration from God
and is useful to teach us what is true
and to make us realize what is wrong in our lives;
it straightens us out and helps us do what is right.
It is God's way of making us well prepared at every point,
fully equipped to do good to everyone.

2 TIMOTHY 3:16-17

BODEGA BAY

There before me lies the mighty ocean,
Teeming with life of every kind, both great and small.
And look! See the ships!
And over there, the whale you made to play in the sea.
Every one of these depends on you to give them daily
food.
You supply it, and they gather it.
You open wide your hand to feed them
and they are satisfied with all your bountiful provision.

PSALM 104:25-28

Hands Across
the Water

AUGUST 1968

Somewhere over the Atlantic Ocean

I peer out the little oval window into the clouds, searching for the coastline. Still in a state of disbelief, I try to discern the transitional point in my life that brought me out of a small town in northern Idaho into this moment and this airplane as it prepares for the approach to Heathrow Airport, London, England, Europe—the Beatles!

Less than a year after the death of manager Brian Epstein, the Beatles are masterminding their own business empire, Apple Industries. Ron Kass, the president of Apple Industries, notified Stanley Gortikov, the president of Capitol Industries, that he and the "lads" are considering asking me to become the U.S. manager of their record division, Apple Records. They asked that I join them in London for a dramatic and insightful series of Apple-related meetings. It seems that washing my feet, brushing the potato peels out of my hair, working my way through college, and then scrambling my way up through the corporate ranks at Capitol Records, Hollywood, is paying off in a way I never imagined. I still have a hard time extricating myself from the small-town country boy within: dust to above the ankles, dirt roads, rolling hills, quiet

JULY 1968
LONDON

Apple moves into new offices at 3 Savile Row.

The Beatles attend the world premiere of the animated film Yellow Submarine *at the London Pavilion.*

Work on their new album, The Beatles *(referred to worldwide as* the White Album*), continues at EMI and Trident Studios. This immense recording project was started at George's Esher Surrey home studio in May, and at this point, stood at about a dozen songs in various stages of completion.*

The Beatles close down their Baker Street Apple Boutique. The one on Kings Road suffered the same defeat a few weeks later.

fields, and simple surroundings. This world is precisely 6,071 miles and just as many light years away from my Idaho beginnings and the Nez Perce Indian reservation lands where I grew up—a world with no freebies, no frills, no backstage passes, no fish and chips wrapped in newspaper, no bobbies on horseback, no afternoon teas, and certainly no Fab Four.

As I continue to gaze out the window, the airplane becomes a reverse time capsule as we fall together into my destiny:

I'm traveling with Stanley Gortikov and Capitol's head of Press and Publicity, Larry Delaney. Apple A&R man, Peter Asher (of Peter and Gordon fame and an old friend of mine by now), is scheduled to pick us up at London's Heathrow Airport. Gortikov's straightforward admonition on the way to LAX (Los Angeles International Airport)— that the Beatles currently account for approximately 50 percent of Capitol's business—keeps running through my head. Fifty percent! As he subtly puts it, "When it has to do with the Beatles—*there is no margin for error.*"

At the Capitol Tower back in Hollywood after our trip, Bob York, my immediate superior and the VP general manager of the company, summons me into his office to discuss my new responsibilities and to let me know in no uncertain terms that I am to "keep it together" as far as the Beatles and the Apple staffers are concerned. In order to make my job easier, he informs me that I do not have to get approvals for my travel, expenditures, or schedules. In fact, I will not even be required to explain my whereabouts or what I am doing—as long as I "keep it together"! At this point, I expect Glen Wallichs, the founder and chairman of the board of Capitol, to call me over to his home next and instruct me to "keep it together" with the Beatles just to be sure I get the message from the complete executive hierarchy of the company! I do get the message, but more than that, Capitol Records has just handed me a first-class ticket to ride on a long and wonderfully winding road into the most amazing place and time in musical history.

I stop dream-staring out the window and begin straining to see land. Suddenly, I see sparkling lights way off and way down below; I'm seeing

AUGUST 1968
LOS ANGELES

In response to an invitation by the Beatles, Stanley Gortikov, president of Capitol Industries; along with Ken Mansfield, national promotion manager-director of Artist Relations; and Larry Delaney, press and publicity chief for the label, fly to London to begin strategy meetings pertaining to the release of Apple Records' product in the U.S.A.

Upon return to Los Angeles, Mansfield is promoted to Capitol's Director of Independent Labels, and the Beatles and Ron Kass select him to be their U.S. manager of Apple Records.

England for the first time! Then I realize that because we have taken the typical north-southeast approach, we are being blessed with a night view of portions of Scotland, Ireland, and northern England. The stewardess shakes me out of my wonderment and asks if I want coffee or tea with my breakfast. "Coffee please...no wait, I'll have tea." I better get used to it!

I twist off the wind tunnel of air above me and pull close the thin excuse for a blanket. My body remains in an odd angular relationship to the seat so that I can still search for the coastline. I feel like a kid: wrapped in a blanket, excited, nervous, and gawking out the window like I have never been on an airplane before.

As the runway comes into sight, the view from the oval window looks cold, rainy, and bleak.

God, I am scared.

The Apple Meetings. *Using George as the common point, the layout of the partici-pants in the hotel suite becomes apparent in these two pictures. It still seems odd to me that at least one of these megamoney groups—Apple or Capitol or the Beatles—couldn't have afforded a larger suite for these meetings. It does speak for the purity of purpose within the Beatles' hearts, however. Besides, the long meetings in close proximity like this did help draw us closer together. (above, l-r) Back of George's Head, Ron Kass, Paul, Ken, Ringo, Stan Gortikov, Mal Evans, John's head in lower right-hand corner. (left, l-r) Larry Delaney, Neil Aspinall, Peter Asher, and George.*

Lost at Sea

JUNE 1995
TWENTY-SEVEN YEARS LATER

Bodega Bay, California

There is something incredibly lonely about the ocean. Its vastness, emptiness, depth, and immense proportions are absolutely overwhelming at times. My perceived self-importance becomes quickly reduced in direct relationship to my contemplation of its grandeur. Its beauty is unmatched, yet that in itself lies diminished by the power that surges forth out of the heart of its very existence. The passage of time and the distance of purpose have cast me upon these uncertain shores, a million memories away from the cities, concerts, crowds, and careening choruses that filled and fueled my heart and hopes for over a third of a century. The applause has grown still with age and the fading stars no longer come out at night, leaving me to face the future of my past reluctantly subdued and at peace. At this point I am somehow expecting the proverbial fat lady to come running out onto the beach singing loudly, kicking sand in the air while clutching a torn backstage pass to her abundant and heaving chest.

Now a wondering warrior, I am left to stand here on the very edge of the world like a brazened bullfighter challenging a gracious beast that at any moment could relegate me and all my frailties into unfathomed nothingness.

Like the songs I once loved, I find that there is a rhythm to the movement of the waves as they explore the shore. They offer forth both a welcome and an implied inaccessibility that puts their allure into the dream realm. They beckon until I feel as if I could be a part of them, and yet, they are so compelling and aloof that I can't even imagine touching them. The ocean dictates authority and withdraws into submission all at the same time. It calls and defers unabashedly into perchance exuberance. To love the ocean is like attaching your emotions to a waif that wanders at will, nonchalantly beckoning while ignoring your sensibilities and weaknesses. It summons and rejects in the same sweeping motion. It soothes and destroys in a singular complex movement. It offers only cold indifference while warmly alluding to everything good that has ever dwelled within its depths. Finally, God's very essence comes pouring forth as I offer my confession before its elegance in a cleansing moment of repentance and humility.

As in life, I feel like a pretender when I come before the judgment of the shore. It ignores me and dictates to me simultaneously. I am in control because I can walk away at will, yet it demeans me in its subtlety. I come before the waves to weep and wonder, to rejoice and request, to laugh and let go. It is here because it is; I am here because I am drawn.

Like the woman I love, it smells and feels good to me. Like her, there are certain things I can depend on, things that will never change or go away. There are also things that I deem crucially important, and they cause me to reconsider and become more forgiving of the things that displease me. I begin to drift and eventually count it all of no account except for the God I worship, the woman I love, and the children that are the blood of my blood. I succumb at the sea edge to the inevitability of this mysterious perpetual exchange: I look down and the waves are touching my soles; I look up and his Word is touching my soul.

Most of all, I become filled with love as I kneel before the tide lines. I think of God almost without ceasing whenever I am within striking distance of the coast. His way is one of unquestioning acceptance. He asks so little and gives so much. He gives the most and gives it first. When I am able to look past myself and get a glimpse of his greatness, I can't help but sense that I have fallen into his uplifting grace and stumbled skyward into the deepest and greatest relationship on Earth.

If only for a minute he could look down from above as I pass before his gaze and say, "This is my child, in whom I am well pleased"—oh! that would be a day of celebration, my happiest day of all! The very thought of being pleasing to Almighty God....

Suddenly I realize the chill around my ankles is the cold water of a rising tide. I face the sunset and feel the warmth of his loving hands on my shoulders; I listen quietly as he speaks silent words of blessed assurance into my waiting heart. Once again adrift in meditation, I have become lost at sea.

The tide and I withdraw from the shore in unison, both retreating into his eternal purpose. The in-between of getting to the here from the there of my life is a blatant blur by his design.

As I ease to the east, I wonder to the west what lies in store for me tomorrow; the tide ebbs in obedience to its eternal purpose and doesn't give it a thought.

I do know that we will all be here in the morning.

A thousand years are but as yesterday to you! They are like a single hour! We glide along the tides of time as swiftly as a racing river, and vanish as quickly as a dream.

PSALM 90:4-5

'50s Rock and Roll

SEPTEMBER/OCTOBER 1990

FIVE YEARS EARLIER

Beverly Hills, California
"Sooo—when are you writing your book?"

I looked across the table into the face of a very familiar but much different Ringo Starr from the Ringo I first met more than twenty-five years ago. His features had deepened yet seemed to have softened with the passing years. We last saw each other about four years earlier here in Los Angeles but under much different circumstances.

At that time, Ringo and his wife, Barbara Bach, had decided to leave L.A., so Ringo invited a few old friends over for a goodbye get-together. As the evening eased to an end, Ringo, Harry Nilsson, Alan Pariser, Timothy Leary, and I were standing in a semicircle in front of the fireplace in his den. Our ladies were in the other room with Barbara. We were winding down our recollections of how we had all met when suddenly Ringo and I realized that we were staring at each other. We both knew what was happening. We were searching familiar faces looking for the two young fellows we had met a quarter of a century earlier. I love the hardy Englishman loyalty to old friendships that prompted him to say warmly for my benefit before the small gathering, "But I've known you the longest, Ken."

For a transcendent portion of the last fifty years, we had both done about as much to our bodies, minds, spirits, and lives as we could with the plethora of drugs and "fast lane" living that was at our disposal for so long. I left Apple in late 1969, but Ringo and I had kept in touch over the years, keeping mutual friends and traditionally sharing the New Years' Eve ritual during the times we both lived in "Lost" Angeles. Eventually things began unraveling for both of us, on different levels, as the '80s wound down. We each bailed out of Hollyweird: Ringo via the Sierra Tucson Rehabilitation Clinic in Arizona on the way to his "Rocca Bella" digs in Monte Carlo, while I flew upwind in that wintertime period of my life and took the northern route along California's rugged Mendocino coast. After an ill-fated layover there, I made a sharp right turn, eventually crash landing in Nashville, Tennessee. Like a sorry gutted goose, I migrated southward, back into the "night life" weakened arms of my old "outlaw" cowboy friends for a much needed soft landing into familiar territory.

But back to Ringo's question. "My book? Well...I have had a lot of offers," I replied, "but my memories aren't quite sleazy enough, and that is all everybody is looking for!"

"Why don't you just make things up?" he offered. "That's what the rest of them have done!" The wry look on his face was one of both helpless consternation and gentle acceptance of so-called "insiders" and their literary distortion of the Beatles, both historically and as individuals. He framed all this with a suggested shrug of the shoulders and an implied "What the hey, I'm used to it" toss of the head.

Ringo and Ken

"Oddly enough," I told him, "my memories of the Apple days and my times with the Beatles are more like scenes from *A Hard Day's Night* or *Help!* That is really how I see the period of time I spent with the four of you. In fact, I always had the feeling that you guys presented a certain 'proper' and upbeat side to me so that I would be impressed with the great business sense you had in running Apple. I felt you were putting on this contrivance so I could see how together you all were. I had it all figured out that you wanted me to be enthused with the great Apple enterprises so that after a few days at 3 Savile Row, I would be sent back to the States pumped, hustled, and primed—totally ready to really go to work for you."

Ringo cocked his head as he shot a sideways glance to our mutual, longtime friend and attorney Bruce Grakal, who had joined us for this little reunion. (I had known both of them long before they had met and yet, ironically, had nothing to do with introducing them or establishing their business relationship.) I had learned over the years that this

1989

MARCH

Ringo and Buck Owens re-record "Act Naturally."

AUGUST

Ringo obtains restraining order in an Atlanta court barring Chips Moman and CRS Records from releasing a project recorded in Memphis two years earlier.

particular version of Ringo's collection of many animated looks meant that somewhere soon in this conversation I was going to be the recipient of a Beatlestyle barb, the type that he and the other "lads" made famous over the years during interviews and press conferences. (Ringo always gave new dimension to the term "Starr struck"!)

"Oh yes, Ken, the Beatles really didn't have that much to do in those days. We would just sit around and think of ways that we could act to impress you—sort of an all-out effort by the four of us to convince you that we were important enough to warrant your incredible music industry talents! You know, to this day we still consider your visits as the times of our finest performances!" His delivery of this zinger embarrassed me into the realization of how wrapped up in my own world I had been in the early days. I had actually believed that, just like everything else, even the Beatles world revolved around me.

We were having dinner that night at Portofino, a restaurant in the Beverly Hillcrest Hotel where I was staying. I had called him in Monte Carlo about two weeks earlier with an idea and a business proposition.

He expressed interest and asked if I would fly in from Nashville to discuss things further since he was going to be in Los Angeles for a few days in about two weeks. Fortunately, and coincidentally, I was producing a new record on the legendary "Flying Burrito Brothers" at that time and had wanted to do the mixes in Los Angeles. I agreed, and over the phone we found that we were capable of finalizing arrangements to meet and have a long overdue dinner without the customary aid of agents and managers.

When we met in the lobby, it was obvious that we were curious as to how the other would look. Comparatively speaking, we both looked and felt great. The last time we had seen each other, we both had a lot of room for improvement. Ringo was five feet eight inches tall and weighed only ninety-seven pounds (seven stone). I was five feet nine and so skinny and drawn that I could sit on a dime and you could still read "In God We Trust" around the edges! (Ringo joked during dinner about his new lifestyle: "Now I exercise and play golf. I am free of drugs and alcohol; I eat right, take good care of myself, plus I attend classes. In fact, I've finally become everyone I used to hate!")

We ate, talked, reminisced, and laughed like old school chums. It was simple fun with good simple people. In the '60s I had looked forward to the time when the Beatles "thing" would be over so Ringo and I could just be friends. I always really liked him back then but knew that his intense fame would probably preclude him from being a normal pal with anybody outside of a small group of longtime mates. Because of the fleeting nature of fame, I figured it would all be over someday and then we could just hang out and brag about our "fifteen minutes" and what big deals we all were in the "old days." I had no idea that the Beatles would be an eternal force in rock and roll and the entertainment industry. Even today, more than thirty years later, there is a class difference between a superstar of Beatles proportions and everyone else in this exclusive rock and roll galaxy. To his credit, superstar Ringo has a way of ignoring all that—most of the time.

That night over my Cabernet wine and his cranberry juice, he told me that for the first time in years he was totally free of all contracts. (In other words: Mr. Starkey is open to something new and officially able to do anything he wants. The rock doctor is in!) We agreed that I would represent him to the record companies for his first new album of studio rock and roll in almost a decade. The resulting album became the 1992 Private Music/BMG release *Time Takes Time*. Also that night, I felt that my silence had been noted and honored, and that Ringo had released me to write about my feelings and memories of my time with the Beatles and Apple Records.

My negotiations on Ringo's behalf with Private Music's president Ron Goldstein and label owner Peter Baumann were greatly enhanced by the fact that Ringo had a unique marketing appeal to their company. Private Music had earned a reputation as a successful New Age label, largely due to the success of Yanni and Suzanne Ciani. Baumann, however, wanted more, and decided to open up his vision of becoming a full spectrum pop and contemporary music label. Having one of the Beatles as your calling card into the rock and roll part of this (ad)venture was stepping forward briskly with a pretty heavy opening act—prestige with a capital B. Peter was also smart enough to know that, in time, a Ringo Starr product would have incredible historic value; therefore, he was able to approach the investment musically, strategically, and corporately. Because he was a Beatles fan, he also found the whole idea pleasantly personal.

The whole Private Music relationship began the next day after my dinner with Ringo and Bruce. I flew home to Nashville in the morning and started making calls from my office that afternoon. My first call was right back to L.A.—to Private Music A&R chief Jamie Cohen.

Jamie had recently told me about the internal musical desires at Private Music, and I felt this venture was just what they were looking for. For me, they had all the elements that I felt Ringo needed in a new recording situation. He needed personal attention and expected proper respect for someone of his stature. He was fed up with bad experiences, including a lot of the attitudes of the major label syndrome; but at the same time, he needed the power of a major distribution system. Private Music, by concept, was probably the only totally perfect place for him at that time. They were distributed by powerhouse BMG/RCA (whose president, Joe Galante, was a friend of mine). Private Music was an extremely well-funded, personal, high-class label with great vision and the heart of artist understanding at its very core. Label owner Peter Baumann was a member of the

1990

MAY

Ringo contributes a new recording and video of "I Call Your Name" to the Lennon Scholarship Fund Concert in Liverpool.

SEPTEMBER

Ringo, Ken Mansfield, and attorney Bruce Grakal dine at Portofino in Beverly Hills to discuss production of Ringo's first official studio album since 1983.

1991

MARCH THROUGH SEPTEMBER

Recording begins on new album in six L.A. studios with producers Jeff Lynne, Peter Asher, and Phil Ramone.

internationally acclaimed Tangerine Dream, one of rock's most avant garde and visionary groups. An artist and a European, he was completely dedicated to professionalism in a label that was his own personal and preferential private music! He had wisely selected previous Island Records label topper Ron Goldstein as his president. Goldstein had that same kind of knowledge and class reminiscent of Ron Kass, which made Ringo comfortable. Jamie Cohen had a street edge and rock and roll remembrance that Ringo needed from an A&R executive.

After our brief conversation that afternoon, Jamie became very excited about the opportunity and wanted to talk to Ron and Peter about Ringo. He made me promise not to talk to another record label for twenty-four hours.

I agreed.

The next morning, I walked into my office to an unexpected conference call with the three of them. Peter Baumann was very officious and concise as he graciously informed me that he would like to meet Ringo. I countered in form that of course everyone wants to meet Ringo—after all he was a Beatle! I did add that if he wanted to talk about a record deal, however, I would meet with him first; and if I believed he was serious, then I would set up a meeting with Ringo and Bruce. I added that a sure way for me to know if he was serious was if my travel agent notified me within the next hour that a prepaid first-class round-trip plane ticket was waiting for me at the Nashville airport for an early flight back to L.A. the next morning.

There was.

I went.

He was serious.

I was picked up at LAX, elegantly delivered to a Beverly Hills hotel, and then transported to the Private Music Melrose Avenue executive offices. We spent the entire day in meetings, and then Peter, Ron, Jamie, and I capped the day's discussions with a wonderful dinner at Chaya Beverly Hills. Peter was flying out the next day at about the same time I was returning to Nashville, so we agreed I would meet him at his Bel Air home for breakfast. We would then finish up our conversation and negotiations in his limo on the way to the airport.

Peter and Ken

As planned, I went to Peter's home early the next day, and by morning's end, most of the major deal points had been worked out—subject, of course, to Bruce Grakal's and Ringo's approval. Suddenly I realized we were experiencing a "pregnant pause" and that I was the focal point of a very intent stare. As it was Peter's silent moment, he finally broke it by asking, "OK, Ken, what's Ringo going to cost me?" I was well aware that at this point we had discussed just about everything except the actual dollars for Ringo and the recording budget. I took a deep breath because I knew that this was the time to play my ace. I also knew I had to bring a "winning hand" home to Ringo and Bruce. "Peter," I said as coolly as I possibly could, "the five most popular and famous names ever in the history of the music entertainment industry are Elvis Presley and the four Beatles. Only three of these five gentlemen are still with us. I'm offering Private Music one-third of the most famous entertainers of all time!" He sank slowly back in his leather chair, stroked his chin, and said with a warm sarcastic grin, "This is going to cost me, isn't it?"

I can't disclose the particulars of the financial arrangement we made that day, but I will admit that it was consistent with the bigger-than-life aspect of the world's greatest band. I do know that I will never forget the look on Peter Baumann's face as he attempted to maintain a characteristically unfazed sense of propriety as he pondered the deal.

He agreed to my offer.

He was serious.

(Now, back to that initial dinner with Ringo and Bruce:)

While Bruce and I focused on business and legal structures, Ringo reminisced. "The Beatles were a really great rock and roll band! That is why we made it! Now, once again, I want to make an album with that basic hard-driving essence, but with a larger group of super musicians." He was almost entertaining himself as he began to envision upcoming recording sessions while Bruce and I discussed the parameters of a potential deal. Ringo became more animated as he talked, suggesting potential band members and producers. He glanced periodically at his watch and mumbled something about meeting up later with his wife, Barbara. As he spoke, his words moved back and away in my consciousness, as if in a warm echo chamber. Time and this moment went into slow motion, and I thought to myself that although he looked different now (a full quarter of a century had passed since we had first met), he really hadn't changed at all. I remember sitting on the floor of the basement Apple recording studio during the *Let It Be* sessions. Ringo would periodically stare at his watch as the day drew on into evening and the others were arguing about whatever song they were working on. He was ready to play or go home. As soon as it was decided that the session was

1992

FEBRUARY

Ringo begins more recordings for the new album, with tracks produced by Don Was.

MAY

Time Takes Time is released. Tour and album kickoff party is held at Paramount Studios in Hollywood, California.

over, he was off the drum stool, out of the door, and into the car. In the beginning, middle, and to the very end, I believe that Ringo will always want nothing more than just to play music and then go home and be with those he loves.

Ken, Ron Goldstein, Peter Baumann, and Ringo

Suddenly, all three of us stopped in the middle of the moment. We looked around the table at one another and began laughing. If we had said to ourselves when we were in our twenties that we would be planning Ringo's next rock and roll album when we were in our fifties, not one of us would have ever believed it. Fifties rock and roll! The beat of rock and roll had entered, shaped, and shaken our lives in the '50s. Now we were in our fifties, and there was still that something shaking and beating inside that made us feel like we could rock, and would roll, on forever!

I needed this project; things had been pretty bleak career-wise for a long time.

Ringo knew that.

It was nice to get a little help from a friend!

Kings

DECEMBER 1994
FOUR YEARS LATER

Bodega Bay, California

It's December, and the sandpipers and terns are all but absent from the sea's edge. I miss the activity, the dance, the obtuse concern that they have with the coming and going of the waves. You can almost hear a *symphonie comique* playing behind the sandpipers' scenario as they foolishly scoot and run about, playing tag with the waves. I stare for long periods of time, trying to discern their mission, their purpose, their raison d'être. The terns, on the other hand, know exactly what their mission is at all times. They are here to eat.

It is almost Christmas on the North Coast, and like other times on the edge, it has its own special personality. The sunsets are startling! Sometimes I feel I should drive inland, grab the first unbeliever I find by the nape of the neck, drag them down to the very edge, and make them look westward out to sea. The colors mount and spray above and beyond the horizon in shades of pastel and deep hues that go beyond anything we could even imagine. I would hold their countenance to the unfolding wonder and dare them to deny God and his immense glory.

Although the heavens crescendo in glorious palettes of hues and majesty in the early evening sunsets, I still prefer to venture out and into the bosom of the shore, embraced by the soft morning light. It is so amazing that I can live in this nation's most populous state, dwell in its most special area, and on any given day be by myself on empty miles of long stretches of beach.

Today is one of those days. I never knew there were so many shades of gray. How can this blending of muted blues, pale purples, and subdued whites have so much color and depth? This is real, but yet I sense I am standing in another dimension where color, time, space, and perception appear to elongate until I go gliding into spiritual superspace. Everything goes deeper as I seem to sink and sail at the same time. I can't explain why I feel God's presence here in this place more than anywhere I have ever been before. Every other thought and desire washes away to the west with the tide. Everything I think and feel has to do with him. I watch the people who come to the edge for a vacation, a week, a weekend, a day, an hour, or a minute; and as their faces look outward, you can see their spirit slowly begin looking upward. I love to experience their special joy as they see the sea and feel the salt air heal their souls. Some worship without even knowing.

The few remaining seabirds have deepened in color and are more serious about their tasks by the tides. The deer that feed outside our window each afternoon on the edge of dusk have taken on a darker coat and also seem to have mellowed into the new season. They are not as sociable or playful. They just eat the neighbor's shrubs and then leave.

Because it is winter on the North Coast, everything is different. I think part of the reason it is so easy to feel closer to God here is that his omnipotence is more apparent than in the city or somewhere else inland that offers a more even climate. The powerful winds and torrential rains drive you inside and force you into each other's lives or to face your own thoughts. The storms lift, and you venture forth strictly by its permission. Retreat is inevitable and always on their terms.

Walking with the waves in the winter is like walking in the Word on a daily basis. It is not always as easy as I would like it to be. When I look outside in anticipation of the morning's adventure, I am almost always hesitant to go forth this time of year. It seems so threatening, and I fear discomfort. But I must go, because out there amongst the wind, the waves, the sea grasses, the salt air, and the thundering surf awaits my daily talk with my loving heavenly Father.

I am getting so I can't confess on the couch anymore!

I need to feel him in my face when we talk. I need the awesome, overwhelming example of his magnificent presence in the dunes, the driftwood, the creatures of the edge, the deafening sound of the breakers on the rocks, and the crackle of the foam as it retreats from the sand.

It is abundantly clear—my total nothingness in this setting. I am surrounded with the magnificence and richness of his being. Because I belong to him, I share in his riches. I am an heir to his kingdom.

I am a child of the King, and royal blood surges through my veins. It covers and cleanses me now and for all time. I walk with the King of kings on this stretch of sand. I have entered the holy of holies and am in the presence of royalty. I am wrapped in the warmth of his sovereignty, eternally blessed, sheltered by mercy, and loved unconditionally. I am a child of the King and stand before him in his courtyard again today. I praise him for the beauty that surrounds me and for the beauty that fills every part of me in the form of his Holy Spirit.

Words I don't understand pour forth from lips privileged to say his name. I become lost in his wonder each time I remember that I have been graciously found by his love, saved by his grace.

I am startled by an old friend who has just moved to Bodega Bay from Tennessee. He brought his dog of the South, Bruiser, down to the ocean today for the first time. Bruiser is one of those giant, lovable, yellow Labrador Retrievers that reminds me of God's ways because of his resplendent, unconditional twenty-four-hour-a-day love and faithfulness. Anyway, Bruiser, seeing the ocean for the first time, got so excited that he instinctively ran right into it and swam in a perfect line straight out to sea. He had no concept of its vastness or where he was headed. He just knew he wanted to find the very heart of its magnificence. It absolutely astounded me that as soon as his master called out to him, Bruiser heard his voice above the roar of the waves and made an immediate amphibious about-face and swam safely back to shore.

Watching Bruiser made me realize that I have to learn to love God in the same way that he jumped into the ocean. I long to be able just to dive in and head out into his greatness in a straight line like nothing else mattered. I need to learn how to swim toward him with all my heart, even though I have no idea what is just beyond the horizon.

Most of all, I need to be able to hear his voice above the roar of my circumstances!

The peace of God is an eternal calm like the cushion of the sea. It lies so deeply within the human heart that no external difficulty or disturbance can reach it. Anyone who enters the presence of God becomes a partaker of that undisturbed and undisturbable calm.

ARTHUR TAPPAN PIERSON

Eight Arms
To Hold You

AUGUST 1965

TWENTY-NINE YEARS EARLIER

Hollywood, California
Here is how it all began with me and the "lads."

As recently appointed West Coast district promotion manager for Capitol Records, part of my job description included handling all artist relations, activities, concerts, and record promotional matters in the Los Angeles area. The Beatles' 1965 Hollywood Bowl concert and related press conference functionally and geographically fell clearly into that category. Instead of doing computerized cost, budget, and program analysis for the Saturn and Surveyor space programs (my job a few months earlier in San Diego), I was now playing host to the four most famous entertainers in the world. Although the transition was sudden, my own youthful sense of self-importance was so developed that I felt very at ease with the whole assignment. I think if I had had any concept of how historical this all was and how incredibly talented and innovative these guys truly were, I would have probably freaked out!

As it turned out, I was one of the first young American executives they had worked with since their ascension to stratospheric stardom. Up until then, everyone they met in the executive world outside their isolated and insulated realm was either a lord of EMI, a corporate chairman, or something equally as thick and elderly. I was a relatively youthful twenty-seven years old. Talk about being in the right place at the right time! I think that fact combined with my unique head-in-the-sand approach to awareness kept me from being numbed by fanhood. This form of untrammeled aplomb by default must have made me appear more accessible to them.

The Beatles had come to L.A. for two consecutive night concerts at the Hollywood Bowl as part of their 1965 record-breaking tour. The press conference was purposed to promote this fact, to further our (Capitol's) relationship with the media, and to present the band with their gold records for the *Help!* album. You can only imagine the security measures that had to be taken. We held the press conference in our ground floor and biggest recording studio—Studio A. This afforded us one incredible advantage—opening into the back of the main room was a load-in door that was used for carting in instruments and equipment for the recording sessions. By bringing the Beatles to the press conference in an armored car, we were able to back the rig up flush to the back of the building and let the lads disembark directly into the closed studio.

We had set a small riser with a long table and four chairs a matter of a few feet from the load-in door. Brian Epstein was stationed to their left down off the riser (facing the audience), and I was in the same position on the right. We were then flanked by security police. "Roving security" was handled, of course, by Beatle "roadie" Mal Evans, who was everywhere at the same time. He had the incredible ability to completely take care of the business of watching out for the lads and to quietly gather a rather respectable social life for himself while he was at it!

Once the lads were in place on the podium, then the select and elite of the radio/television/printed media along with those with industry clout were allowed into the room. They were carefully controlled and guided in a disguised order of importance to specific seating locations in the rows of chairs that had been set up for the occasion.

George Harrison was positioned at my end of the podium and soon began losing interest in the same old questions. Because I was stationed about two feet to the right and one step down from the makeshift platform, he turned away from the proceedings and began asking me about California in general and Hollywood in specific. He exuded such a casual, boyish, and natural charm that it virtually shined out loud through the din of the star-worship madness that filled the room of "insiders." Eventually, one by one, the other three entered into the conversation when one of the other Beatles was fielding a question. The unabashed innocence in their

manner of questioning me about L.A. further confirmed the existence of this delightful childlike aspect of their basic nature: "Have you ever been to Grauman's Chinese Theater?"; "Are

AUGUST 1965

Beatles appear live on Blackpool Night Out (ABC-TV UK).

Help! *movie is released in U.K.*

Help! *movie opens in New York.*

Beatles fly to U.S.A.

Capitol's Beatles IV *album completes 6 weeks as #1 on* Billboard's *album chart.*

Beatles tape Sept. 12 Ed Sullivan Show season opener.

Beatles open U.S. tour at Shea Stadium in New York.

Beatles fly to L.A. and a stay at 2850 Benedict Canyon Drive.

Capitol Tower press conference where Beatles receive RIAA Gold Record for Help! *LP.*

Two night concerts at the Hollywood Bowl. Shows recorded and finally released in 1977 as part of Beatles Live at the Hollywood Bowl.

Final show of 1965 U.S. tour at San Francisco's Cow Palace.

Ken is positioned to George's right down off the podium while Brian Epstein maintained the same position (just off camera) to Ringo's left.

James Dean's prints there?" (John); "How far is Mullholland Drive from here?" (George); "Do you know Buck Owens, because I would like to meet him while we are here?" (Ringo); "Gene Vincent was on Capitol—can you get me some of his old records?" (Paul); etc.

Finally, they were asked to return their attention to the matter at hand. Paul discretely called Mal over and told him to get my name so that I could come up to the house the next day and continue the conversation. They had a much-deserved week off from the tour and were spending it secluded in a Beverly Hills gated hillside semi-mansion. They needed a "local," and because I was an associate of sorts, it made it all fit for me to spend the day with them.

Little did I know at that time that this invitation would be the first of two. This one brought me to 2850 Benedict Canyon Road, their rented house in L.A., and I had to change my plans in order to go for the day. The next one would bring me to 3 Savile Row, their office building in London, and that would change my life—forever.

Beauty for Ashes

NOVEMBER 1993
TWENTY-EIGHT YEARS LATER

Bodega Bay, California

Sometimes I feel as if I have been washed up on this rugged North Coast shore by a cruel, harsh, and unforgiving sea. My dreams, hopes, plans, and hard work all lie ruined in the bottomless depths of these dark waters I stare at each day. Contrapuntal reflections ebb and flow through my mind like discarded extra verses of songs past. The music has never stopped—but for some reason, I did.

It is almost impossible to look back and determine that precise moment when the winds guiding my voyage shifted. Somewhere between smooth sailing and a pleasure cruise, I was swept off course and suddenly found myself trying to navigate treacherous times and uncharted places. If I had only known God then, I would have had a captain to lead me safely across the ocean. If I had only known Jesus, I would have had a shipmate who could teach me when I was confused, heal me when I was sick, guide me when I was lost, and save me when I was drowning. If only I had been filled with the Holy Spirit in those days, I would have had a comforter for the lonely nights of that wind-tossed journey, an inner peace to shield me from the devastating storms that surrounded my soul.

They are the authors of the map I needed for my journey. I needed a chart, a journal with clear directions, a log to refer to—a guidebook wherein their commands could speak to my wandering spirit. I needed a book so powerful that its very words could burn a living message into the absolute heart of my heart. I needed the irrefutable written holy Word of God, the Father Almighty, the Creator of the very seas I was lost upon! For the greater part of my journey that began the day I set sail from the rugged shores of northern Idaho, I had none of these. Unfortunately, *Billboard* magazine was my Bible; the record charts, my God; and prestigious positions, my purpose. The holy grail was a Grammy, and the best table at the Brown Derby —the promised land.

Since the day I untied the symbolic apron's knot from the mooring of a loving mother's godly instruction, I made my own rules and set my own course. The ship I set sail upon picked up empty cargo at every port. It rotted in the holds of my being until its very nothingness weighed down my voyage so much that only the destruction that lay in its wake remained. The vacuum I was living in created the tempest that tossed me about. The turbulence grew until the beatings upon the hull of my self-determination could no longer weather the storm.

*   *   *   *

Then the most incredible thing happened. As I let go of the rudder of my relentless obstinance and surrendered to the waiting mire that I had sailed into, I felt the rush of living water cover my soul. The Father, the Son, and the Holy Spirit were with me. Not for one moment, ever, had

I been sailing alone! God's hand was always poised, ready
to grab the wheel just before I was going to dash upon the
rocks. He was always there, just waiting to guide me away
from the rocks and to "the Rock"! I know now that he must
have wept in the winds as he reluctantly let me set my own
course long enough to capsize—a loving Father once again
watching his child being broken before the mast. So my
time-gathered ungodly cargo finally sank into the sea with
me still clinging stubbornly to the wreckage. But then, in
the lifeboat of God's mercy, I was washed upon the ever
waiting shore where I came to rest within the glow of his
all-consuming fire.

Then, He gave me beauty for ashes; he gave me a fresh-
water start; and most of all, he gave me everlasting life!

Now I return to the same place on the banks of this safe
harbor and look out across a sea of forgiveness. I wait for his
Word on the whitecaps. I beg to be broken upon the beckoning breakers that will bring a bounty of blessings into an
obedient life. I stand ready to sail away upon the leading bow
of his will into the Son. I seek solace here and find comfort
among the seagulls and the sound of the surf. I search the
shore and find that the waves have washed away all remembrances of the battle that took place here. The beach is washed
clean and so am I. I sit on the sand, wrapped in his mercy and
warmed by his grace.

I marvel at how much more peaceful it is now. My eyes
look to the horizon. Out in the bay, I can see a rock, and my
ears become aware of the roll of the waves. I sense that in
some way in my life, there will always be some kind of rock
and roll.

"In my great trouble I cried to the Lord and he answered me; from the depths of death I called, and Lord, you heard me! You threw me into the ocean depths; I sank down into the floods of waters and was covered by your wild and stormy waves.... 'Oh Lord, you have rejected me and cast me away...'

"I sank beneath the waves, and death was very near. The waters closed above me; the seaweed wrapped itself around my head. I went down to the bottoms of the mountains that rise from off the ocean floor. I was locked out of life and imprisoned in the land of death. But, oh Lord my God, you snatched me from the yawning jaws of death."
Jonah 2:2-6

To all who mourn...he will give: Beauty for ashes; Joy instead of mourning; Praise instead of heaviness.

ISAIAH 61:3

The Fool on the Hill

AUGUST 1965
TWENTY-EIGHT YEARS EARLIER

Benedict Canyon

Monday, August 30, 1965—the day after the Beatles' Hollywood press conference and the first of their two consecutive nights at the Hollywood Bowl—was absolute madness. Happily following up on Paul's invitation and then receiving permission from road manager and general assistant Mal Evans to bring a guest, I invited someone I shall call "Bruce" to accompany me to an afternoon at the house in Benedict Canyon, which had served as refuge for the group since the previous Monday.

Bruce was the young music director at KBLA, the fourth-rated rock and roll station in L.A. I figured if I took him along with me, then Capitol would virtually own the airplay situation at that station, and I did have the recording careers of other label artists besides the Beatles to contend with. KBLA was new and on the bottom of the rock ratings war in L.A., so since only one guest could accompany me to the absolute center of the rock and roll universe that day, this invitation would probably endear me to Bruce forever. Bruce was well aware that I chose him over the heavy hitters at the powerhouse stations, KHJ, KRLA, and KFWB. The politics

Conquering America was the best thing.... We reckoned we could make it because there were four of us. None of us would've made it alone, because Paul wasn't strong enough, I didn't have enough girl appeal, George was too quiet, and Ringo was the drummer. But we thought that everyone would be able to dig at least one of us, and that's how it turned out.

JOHN LENNON

of the situation were even more intense because Bruce's rival, KRLA, was the official host radio station for the Beatles' shows at the Hollywood Bowl. Actually, I was taking a giant risk by inviting Bruce, because if Dick Moreland, my friend and music director at KRLA, the sponsoring station, found out I had asked Bruce instead of him, I could be losing a lot in order to gain a little. (In all honesty, I felt that KBLA was going to move ahead of the other stations in fast order, so my decision wasn't totally based on Bruce's personality or pure ethics.)

The house on the hill was a point of semi-calm engulfed in a residential traffic jam that was surrounded by a frenzied throng. Getting to the gate was an event in itself. By the time we were within twenty-five yards of the entrance and being ushered on ahead, it became clear to the fans that we were going in! That fact alone attracted a misspent form of adoration that led to us giving numerous autographs and receiving many just-let-me-touch-someone-who-is-going-to-touch-a-Beatle prods. (You can imagine what it was like when we left with perceived Beatle touches all over us!)

Once inside, it was like being in the eye of a storm that was under siege around the edges. There were quite a few people there: a bongo player was either jamming with or giving Ringo lessons in a poolside bedroom; some fellow was demonstrating a Fender Bender guitar strap to George; John was on the edge of the pool, head down, intently listening to someone who was obviously pouring forth earthshaking philosophical truisms; Paul was energized and entertained by a small group of industry insiders. A quiet, slender, tanned girl was swimming most of the time without really talking much to anyone. Later on I was introduced to her—Joan Baez.

Most of my attention was drawn to Mal Evans dealing with the onslaught around the edges. Mal and head road manager Neil Aspinall both were amazingly adept at arranging, maneuvering, organizing, and protecting the four lads. They were both confidants and privy to just about everything that went down, somewhat even more so than manager Brian Epstein in the day-to-day Beatle activities. After Brian died and Apple came to fruition, they along with label general manager Jack Oliver and Derek Taylor were virtually the ones who opened the "apple stand" in the morning and shut out the lights at night, long after everyone else had gone home. Even though Mal served as a non-stop jack-of-all-trades that afternoon, the day was the beginning of an incredible friendship between him and me that took us right up to the night of his death a little more than ten years later.

Since the pool was on the hillside of the estate, it was perched on the edge of a forty-foot, slightly slanted stone wall that ran up from the canyon below. Mal was running around the edge of the wall, garden hosing back young people who were trying to scale the abutment. Security guards lined the other ten-foot high fences that surrounded the property where there was a small but steady stream of crashers being picked up from the ground the minute they made it over. Each one was sternly but courteously escorted back outside. Some individual fans had the pleasure of being escorted several times that day. Every now and then, Paul would look over at one of them and smile and wave like they were an old friend. This had an effect comparable to shooting them with a tranquilizer gun. They would bliss out with the recognition and become limp and quiet as they were dragged away and banished to the other side of the fence.

By this time in their careers, the Beatles seemed to have developed an unawareness to anything going on around them except that which was immediately before them and had their attention at that specific time. In all honesty, I still didn't get it. They were such nice guys and so courteous during it all— so normal. Because they seemed unaffected by their fame, I sometimes lost sight of what the attraction was or what it was all about, and in later years, working for them and being with them seemed pretty normal.

Back to KB(ruce)LA: I was wrong on three out of two of the aforementioned counts about my imminently powerful guest. First, KBLA became an even more distant fourth as time rolled on. Second, Bruce wouldn't give me the time of day, let alone airplay after he got to meet the Beatles. Third, he made a fool of himself at the poolside on the hill by becoming a star-glazed fan, hovering and drooling over each Beatle in repeated succession. He then capped the whole thing off by hauling out a pile of KBLA T-shirts for them to autograph!

I drove my guest, who made a fool of himself on the hill, home. However, at that time, you could have fooled me as to the effect the band we had just left behind was going to have on my life.

I was no fool, so I didn't come home empty-handed from the day "on the hill." This is the first personalized item I received from the Beatles. Possession, like so many things, is transient; and this album now occupies a treasured spot in someone else's collection!

Fish Tales

MARCH 1995
THIRTY YEARS LATER

Bodega Bay, California

I go down to the wharf almost every afternoon to get fresh fish for the evening. By fresh, I mean it was caught offshore that very afternoon. There is a fishmarket, deli, and restaurant at the wharf, and you can eat it there or take it home. On warm sunny days, I love to go down to the docks and watch the small boats come in with their fresh catch of the day. In this day of worrying about our food sources, it is great to see your evening meal being loaded off the boat and straight into the back door of the fishmarket.

I am fascinated by the local fishermen who sail out with the tide each day in search of their livelihood. They are a rough, craggy breed who trade the fancy things of life for a cold hard bunk on a smelly little fishing boat just to live and be by the sea. I am inextricably and unequivocally drawn to the ocean! I romanticize this attraction and thank God every day for putting this desire and appreciation in me and then graciously placing me here on the very edge. Yet even so, I stand down in awe of these fishermen; they have a love for the sea beyond anything I could imagine! Soon, I am lost in the incredibility and immensity of the passion, provision, and peace of this place. I then become overwhelmed by God's love as it swirls in and about and all around these things. At this point, I usually come out of some kind of ethereal trance and realize that I have stopped in my tracks again, somewhere on the dock, always facing out to sea. I quickly glance at my watch to see how long I have been standing there this time. I become immersed in the smells, the sounds, the creatures, and in watching the people who are drawn here. We may not be special or unusual, but places like this definitely are!

Once again I face the water, and warm feelings of good fortune well up inside me as I reflect on the travel and travail that have brought me to this place. Without thinking or hesitation, I begin to pray out loud from the edge of the pier looking out to the sea before me:

> *Oh, Father God, in your mercy and grace please let me stay here– let me stay in this place within your provision and your will. Keep me safe beside these waters, living the rest of my days within the purpose and intent of your Holy Word. If I must leave here, please grant me your blessed assurance that your hand is on me, that I may hear your Word within me so that I will know that I have come to a new place that is pleasing to you. If I must leave, let me carry the smell and memory of this moment like a sailor who carries a picture of a loved one next to his heart as he ventures out to sea.*

I walk away from the docks, hands in pockets like a shuffling child. I feel great. The bystanders all think this is Bodega Bay. They stare and wonder after this man with the crazy smile on his face who stands on the end of the wharf and talks out to sea. If they only knew! God and I just had a conversation here on the docks beside the Sea of Galilee.

*Oh Lord, you have exam-
ined my heart and know
everything about me. You
know when I sit or stand.
When far away you know
my every thought. You
chart the path ahead of me,
and tell me where to stop
and rest. Every moment,
you know where I am. You
know what I am going to
say before I even say it. You
both precede and follow
me, and place your hand of
blessing on my head....*

*If I ride the morning winds
to the farthest oceans, even
there your hand will guide
me, your strength will
support me.*

PSALM 139:1-5, 9-10

Like Peggy Lee Said: "IS THAT ALL THERE IS?"

1964–1968
ABOUT THIRTY YEARS EARLIER

San Diego–Los Angeles

I will never forget the first time I heard a Beatles record. I was driving down Mission Boulevard in San Diego, California, listening to a local Top 40 station on my way to my consulting job with a firm that specialized in computerized program evaluation and research technique planning for the space industry. It was winter 1964, and I had heard so much about this new group that I was anxious to hear them. Suddenly, the disc jockey front-announced the next record: "I Want to Hold Your Hand." After the record was over, I remember being singularly nonplussed, to say the least. At the most, I couldn't figure what the big deal was all about. Oddly enough, though, I was in awe, but not of that particular record. I was moved by something I couldn't put my finger on, but it didn't really matter because I had my hands too full with a current assignment to spare any part of my mind or fingers anyway. Still, I remember thinking after I heard the record, "Is that it? Is that all there is?" Later on, when, ironically, I ended up working with and for the Beatles, this initial nonplussed reaction was still my basic operative impression. I think that is why it was always so relaxed and natural for me to be involved with them.

FEBRUARY 1964

Beatles arrive in New York City for first visit to U.S.A. "I Want to Hold Your Hand" is already into its seven week run at #1 out of fifteen weeks on the Billboard *charts.*

Beatles tape third-to-be broadcast Ed Sullivan Show *appearance, and then, that same evening, appear live on the program in front of seventy-three million viewers.*

First U.S. concert appearance at New York's Carnegie Hall. Beatles make second appearance on Ed Sullivan Show, *live from Miami.*

I will admit, though, that I have not always been able to maintain such a cool, casual demeanor when working with superstars. Around the same time that my involvement with the Beatles began, I was called upstairs to the E floor by Capitol Industries president Stanley Gortikov. (E stood for "executive" and that floor was the "ivory" portion of the Capitol Tower. It actually was the thirteenth floor, but no one called it that!) I was assigned to spend the day with Judy Garland in her San Francisco penthouse suite in order to coordinate promotional matters surrounding the launch of the famous "live" duet album that she recorded at the London Palladium with daughter Liza Minnelli. I could not believe I was going to spend the day with Judy Garland!

I have zero memory of leaving Stanley Gortikov's office, finishing my workday, going home for the night, packing, driving to LAX, flying to San Francisco, catching a cab, or anything else until I was let into her penthouse digs at the Fairmont Hotel by some stuffy butler/protector-type. I was with Judy Garland—and boy did she treat me like used dirt! She ordered me around, ignored me, yelled at me, didn't acknowledge my presence, acted like she could not stand my presence, and yet all I knew was that I was with Judy Garland—no, I was with Dorothy from Oz! That was one of my most exciting days in the music business. I had spent the day with Judy Garland! Afterward, back in L.A., people would ask me how it went working with Judy Garland. I would smile importantly and answer, "Great!"

It seems funny to me now as I look back, but I was not really excited when I first got to work with the Beatles. I was already working with famous acts every day, many of whom I was a big fan when I was growing up—Stan Kenton, Peggy Lee, George Shearing, Frankie Laine, and the Four Freshmen—plus contemporary acts such as the Beach Boys, Lou Rawls, Nancy Wilson, Bobby Darin, Bobby Rydell, and Al Martino—all big stars in those days. Also, the English onslaught had begun at Capitol—The Seekers (actually Australian), Peter and Gordon, Cilla Black, etc. So the Beatles were just added responsibility and part of the job. As the days, months, and years passed, I would also work simultaneously with other Capitol acts such as The Band, Quicksilver Messenger Service, Bob Seger, Bobbie Gentry, Steve Miller Band, and Glen Campbell, to name a few. (I almost left out Mrs. Miller—actually that is another book in itself!) I grew into my awareness of the Beatles' genius over a period of time, and because of this, ended up with possibly a deeper reverence than most. In other words, I was never infatuated with them—I slowly fell in love with them and their artistry over the years.

Part of this unawareness may have developed out of my promotion-man mentality at the time. You didn't promote a Beatles record—you just hung on when one came out! While I was busy living in the trenches with my other artists, trying to get their records played, I was also spending half my time trying to keep stations from playing advanced copies of new Beatles releases until all the stations could get serviced. I remember the August 1966 release of the *Revolver* album, in particular, as being one of my roughest releases. I spent weeks trying to get a new Glen Campbell record on a major station only to have it taken off the air and thrown out the door at me just because the "other" station across town got the Beatles first.

I doubt that anyone outside the very heart of the record business could even imagine what it was like at that time for promotion men at all labels when a new Beatles record was released. First, it immediately knocked competing records out of the coveted No. 1 spot. Every artist, producer, song-writer, manager, etc. lives to get a No. 1 record. Climbing all the way into the Top 5 or even the No. 2 slot on the national *Billboard* chart is an incredible feat, but like an Olympic medal, it is only the gold medal that really counts in the long run. Having a No. 1 record is the whole big deal! Second, and most importantly, once a new Beatles record was released and took over the No. 1 slot, no other record could get into the spot, even for one week. The sad part of this scenario is that a lot of artists during those years had legitimate No. 1 records but had to settle for the No. 2 or lower position because of the Beatles' dominance of the top chart positions. This not only affected our competition, but our own (Capitol) artists suffered the same fate. You can imagine the artist relations problems I had at Capitol with some of the pretty important stars on our roster.

It seemed that when a Beatle record was released, all other artists' records and airplay "revolved" around what little time was left aside from the Beatles' airplay. Revolver was especially well received by the radio stations, and I felt like I had a gun to my head by suffering stations when unauthorized "exclusive" advance airplay started on this classic work. I would then walk out of the offended station, after trying to make amends, and into the waiting arms of the screaming managers and agents of my other unfortunate, unplayed artists that were also on Capitol. I received this autographed copy unsolicited from England.>

Third, the problem for our other artists went even deeper than that because, as in the unisolated case of Glen Campbell, Capitol artists were constantly being punished for sins they didn't commit. Listener ratings are everything

MARCH 1964

Back in London, Beatles begin shooting first feature film, later to be titled A Hard Day's Night.

to the financial health of a radio station, and when one station got an advance copy of a Beatles record in those days, they immediately garnered approximately 99.99999 percent of the listening audience until their competitor could get their own copy. Plus, when a station did get an exclusive on a Beatles record, they kept announcing their call letters over the song while they were playing it so the other stations couldn't copy it off the air and then turn around and play it on their station. Sometimes this gap between stations having or not having a new Beatles release was a couple of hours or just a few minutes. That was not the point. Even if a station got the record only thirty seconds before its rival, they would scream their exclusive success, proclaim their dominance over their competitor, and announce themselves as the station where you hear the Beatles first. This assured listener loyalty and high ratings for quite some time.

Of course, the losing stations in these battles then held calm, intellectual staff meetings to decide what to do when they were beaten by their competitors. Oddly enough, every station nationwide always came up with one of two "sophisticated" solutions: (a) take all other Capitol artists' records off the playlist and throw them out of the window into the street, or (b) call the local promotion man over to the station and have him stand in the music director's office and watch his artists' records being thrown out the window into the streets. When this happened, my job as both national promotion manager and head of the artist relations department would take an abrupt turn into a living nightmare. The artists, publicists, managers, agents, publishers, and even family members would all descend upon me (or my helpless secretary) demanding an explanation. Of course, I didn't have time to respond because upper management needed to see me so I could explain how this kept happening. Of course, I didn't have time to make these explanations either, because in addition to losing across-the-board airplay on all my artists, I had to deal with irate music directors and station managers. In the midst of this, I was trying to get my helpless local promotion man a copy of the pirated Beatles record so he could salvage a little of his results of years of credibility and relationship building that was his lifeblood.

It was almost impossible to maintain complete security over the release of a Beatles record. There are just too many links in the chain of events that any record goes through before it is released. It only took one minimum-wage worker at one of the mechanical levels of production, reproduction, manufacturing, storage, packaging, shipping, or any other phase to accept a bribe equal to a few month's wages, and the whole nightmare was off and running. I couldn't coordinate simultaneous delivery times to the stations because copies of the records would always leak out and a station would get it before I could get it to everyone at the same time. We tried everything, but nothing worked until I came up with something that was amazingly simple and logical. Best of all, this plan provided a great long-term plan for all Beatles releases.

Here is how it worked: The idea was to eliminate the crucial element in this whole dilemma—the importance of getting the record first. I informed the stations that in the future, a specific time and date for airplay on all new Beatles releases would be set well in advance so that every radio station in the nation would debut the record at exactly the same second regardless of the station size, the market it was in, or the time zone. We would supply the record to all stations well in advance of this target time. Therefore, stations wouldn't have to worry about their competitor playing it first. If another station did jump the gun, then the cooperating station would be able to recover immediately because Capitol (now the good guy) had supplied them a copy for their protection.

If this sounds too simplistic and idealistic, let me explain why this plan did have teeth and did indeed work. If a station chose to ignore our designated airtime and played the copy of the record that we supplied to them ahead of time (or a pirated copy), then not only would their advantage be lost—since the other stations had a copy for immediate response—but in the future, the noncomplying station would not receive the advance copy of the next new Beatles record. So in order for a station to be first one time on a Beatles record, they faced the potential future of being last on every record thereafter—unless they could figure out how to get and pay for a pirated copy for every succeeding record. (Which, by the way, happened to be illegal and actually opened them up to other problems.) If a station did get a pirated copy before we had supplied them or the other stations, they still only had a one-time advantage and would be subject to being left out from then on. The playing field was definitely leveled, and this procedure worked—I only wish I had thought of it a lot earlier.

The first day we put the plan into effect, I found myself once again driving down the freeway listening to a new Beatles record on the car radio. The rock and roll irony of this scenario is that this was where I first heard a Beatles record—but now I was the one deciding when a Beatles record would be played on the radio.

As I listened, I still wondered what it was all about; this time, however, there was a lot more on my mind than "Is that all there is?"

Just Like Jeremiah

SEPTEMBER 1993
ALMOST THIRTY YEARS LATER

Bodega Bay, California

I know a man is not supposed to cry, but today I felt like Jeremiah, the weeping prophet. I wept in the wind as I walked before the waves—wondering why Matt died. I gazed out at the sea, knowing beneath its surface that the sharks and the dolphins swim in the same water. Just once, though, I wish that Flipper could give Jaws a whale of a beating!

Matt was a Christian brother and the young father of three small children. A fourth child was due in a few weeks. He had lost his job recently, and things were tough on all fronts. He was killed instantly in a tragic motorcycle accident. I honestly believe that some of the tears I shed were for those last days that his family had with him. I wish things could have been better before he went away—for the sake of their memories.

I never cried when my dad passed away. I kept thinking I would but...now I can't stop crying for Matt. Maybe I am shedding the tears for this father as a symbol of all fathers when I think about these young children and what they have lost. I fall to my knees at the water's edge and lift my swollen eyes to the heavens above and pray:

*Oh Father God, I know we have special privilege when
we pray for our Christian brothers and sisters. I stand
on your promise now and ask you to put your arms
around these beautiful people. Hold them close —
very close. Fill them with your blessed assurance and
remind them that you are the Father to the fatherless.
Fill their lives with provision and joy. Keep them safe
and strong.*

It is so incredible being a member of Christ's family and
to see the church put its arms around its children. The support
system is automatic as love, food, assistance, and financial
help pours out in abundance. But I start to cry again knowing
that time will pass, attention will diminish, and Matt's wife
and babies will be left to face a long, lonely, hard battle.

I came to the water's edge for answers after I heard the
tragic news today. I have been staring at it for hours—and
waiting. As the ripples wash up on the sand, I want to rush
in and have this whole thing healed, to have everyone's
pain go away, but I stand transfixed, unable to move in
any direction—mentally, physically, or spiritually. I refuse
to ask God why these things happen. He is God—we got
that straight a long time ago—so I have learned to ask
him what and how instead. What am I to learn from this
experience? What can I do that would be in line with his
wishes and purposes? How can I bear a godly witness in a
situation like this, especially when all the unbelievers have
a field day as we "crazy Christians" try to explain this one
away? How can I minister to those in need? How can I
glorify God in this and in every situation in my life?

I suddenly realize that the water has turned blue-black;
it is late, and I am cold and without a jacket. As I walk away
in the deepening dusk, I sense my sorrow gently lift away.

I know down inside where I know things that it isn't the answers and explanations that are important—it is just making sure we know where to go to ask the questions.

The chill on my bare arms goes away, and I feel pulled into a warm place—I think he just put his arms around me too!

No wonder I cry so much!

Oh, that my eyes were a fountain of tears; I would weep forever; I would sob day and night for the slain of my people!

JEREMIAH 9:1

Hollywood
Paul 'E Would

JUNE 1968
TWENTY-FIVE YEARS EARLIER

Los Angeles

When the Apple Records label was conceived, everyone, including the other major labels, initially and incorrectly assumed that it would be distributed by Capitol Records. In actuality, Capitol had no more rights to distribute the label than anyone else. We actually had to compete with the other majors for this prize. We did have one small advantage though; the Beatles were Capitol artists, and distributing Apple through Capitol Records was the only way the Beatles were ever going to be on their own label. This fact, coupled with rather substantial pre-established relationships and a common parent company (EMI), did give us a slight edge! By distributing Apple through Capitol, the Beatles were able to have "Hey Jude" as Apple's debut single release. Technically, the Beatles were not Apple artists. Although they released their records on the Apple label, the controlling documents, contracts, accounting, and record numbers were Capitol's.

We had a convenient coincidence working in our favor once the decision was made that Capitol would distribute Apple. We were getting ready to hold our annual convention in Los Angeles, scheduled for the third week of June 1968.

MAY 1968

On May 30, "Revolution 1"
becomes first song recorded
for what is to be known as
the White Album.

Every salesman, field representative, district and divisional branch manager, as well as all promotion and field merchandising managers were going to be in one room at the same time. In addition, all the major executives and employees from the Tower[1] would be in attendance.

Wouldn't it be great if one of the Beatles were to come to the convention? After all, it was a fairly standard occurrence that when a major distribution deal is made with a new label, one of the owners would almost always appear to announce the new business relationship.

Which Beatle could we get?

Who would come to Hollywood?

Stanley Gortikov called and inquired.

Paul said 'e would!

Paul, 'e would come to Hollywood!

We "snuck" Paul into town without anyone knowing. No one except Gortikov, the upper upper echelon, and I knew that we would be distributing Apple records. Gortikov set the stage by

---

1   Capitol Industries' main offices were located just off Hollywood Boulevard and Vine Street in Hollywood, California. Nicknamed the "Tower," this building housed the major executives and creative personnel who ran the company. Originally designed to look like a stack of records, the finished product was not aesthetically pleasing. Window treatments and the "sun dial" or "needle" on top were added later to give it dimension and alleviate the unplanned squatness of the building. At first, working in that building is a little unusual in that furniture never quite fits right on the slightly curved outside wall of your office. There was also something symmetrically and psychologically unsettling about having an office with no square corners!

announcing that we were going to have a special guest make a big announcement at the convention as a prelim excitement teaser. I don't think anyone ever imagined that it was about Apple and would be made in person by a Beatle.

The convention was in progress, and the big day, Friday, June 21, arrived. Virtually every employee of any import was seated, awaiting the festivities. It was totally dark in the auditorium. We secreted Paul from a holding suite at the Century Plaza Hotel to the convention room. As he started walking down the aisle from the back of the auditorium, a stagehand brought the room lights up slowly. A long gasp came out of the gathering as they began to realize that a real live "in person" Beatle had walked into their midst. Paul, ever the diplomat, began waving, smiling, shaking hands, and giving 1960s-type high fives as he made his way to the stage. Simultaneously, as if by some cosmic cue, everyone started cheering, clapping, standing up, and shouting with joy. There was this incredible feeling of mutual affection between the men and women of Capitol Records and Paul McCartney. I stress mutual because it was a joy equally shared. The left and right brains of a phenomenon in the music business journey had come face-to-face. This was a case where "them that makes the records" got to meet "them that breaks the records." Paul was a member of the group that had given these men and women great prestige, honor, and financial rewards in their professional and personal lives; and they were there before him, the men and women who had brought it all home for the Beatles in America. It was so English and so American—pride and hard work all mixed into an internationally cowritten song entitled "a job well done."

Capitol Records U.S.A. had done a great job for the Beatles. There was no debating that America was the most important market for them to break into. Looking back now, it would seem automatic; after all, they were the Beatles! But one must remember that acceptance in the United States was not a given in those days, and many famous European acts before them had faced dismal failure in the land of American milk and honey. In fact, because Capitol Records was an EMI company and had first right of refusal on all foreign EMI acts for the United States, we had actually passed on the Beatles more than once! Nonetheless, Paul was aware of and thankful for the job that had ultimately been done here. As for the Capitol employees, because of a quota/commission system that was in place at that time, every one of these men and women became relatively wealthy in just one year, until the system was revised downward to take into account the incredible Beatles sales volume. The Beatles had essentially bought them new cars, paid off mortgages, and established their kids' college funds.

When the Capitol "gang" quieted down, Paul made the announcement about Apple. The place went absolutely crazy!

Later, Paul attended an outside cocktail party at the Century Plaza Hotel where he spent time with the field sales/promo/merchandising employees—taking pictures with each one, chatting with them, sharing his fame in an exquisitely common manner that endeared him and his bandmates to this group of hard-working people forever. (They still talk about that afternoon to this day.) Paul rewarded their efforts with this encounter, and as a new record company co-president, he was accomplishing a powerful public relations push in a hands-on manner by enlisting and then fueling their enthusiasm for our new label—Apple Records. When they returned to their homes across the American landscape, you can imagine the effort they put forth to launch the new Apple venture.

A foreshadowing of the feelings and camaraderie that was to be experienced that day occurred when I was bringing Paul down the hallway from his suite to the convention hall. Just prior to the convention, I had returned from Atlanta after hiring an African-American class ring and Bible salesman to head up Capitol's R&B promotion for the Southern states. His name was Sydney Miller, and he had one of those personalities that lit up a room when he walked in. Everyone immediately liked Sydney. He would give the biggest, and to this day I believe, the most sincere smile upon meeting you; then Sydney would own you within minutes. He soon became one of my best men and a loyal friend. I had a sense about hiring new employees, and I knew from the beginning he would be a star on my staff horizon. (Good men working under you always make you look good to the people over you.) Sydney had an amazingly unique and powerful sense of self, and he offered that into his relationships. That was why he made everyone glad to be around him.

JUNE 1968

Sgt. Pepper *still in* Billboard's *album charts more than one year after its release.*

Magical Mystery Tour *is still in* Billboard's *Top 50 almost six months after release.*

George and Ringo visit L.A. June 7–18.

Paul travels to L.A. on June 20.

Paul records "Thingumybob" with Black Dyke Mills Band on June 30.

Anyway, he had gone to his room to get something during the break and was returning down the hall at the same time we came out of Paul's suite. The two came face-to-face, and when Sydney saw Paul, his eyes got as big as saucers, and he started grinning the happiest look I had ever seen. Paul had no idea who Sydney was or that he was a Capitol Records employee—all he knew was that he was standing face to face with this smiling, joyful black dude in the hallway of an L.A. hotel. Spontaneously, they embraced, neither saying a word. Sydney walked away in a daze, and Paul had a serene look on his face before falling back in step, still looking over his shoulder at Sydney dancing down the hall. It was simple respect and human nature at its finest. This was that golden thread that ran through the Beatles' nature and personal makeup—the thread that binds us all together when we get past all the stuff that conditioning imposes upon our natural goodness and love for each other.

The day ended with a round of meetings and dinner and then back to the hotel. I had booked a bungalow for Paul at the Beverly Hills Hotel so he would have privacy and an atmosphere conducive to writing songs for the White Album, the recording of which he had just left behind in London for a few days.

We entered the lobby of the hotel through the front, and Paul stopped at the desk to pick up messages. A young boy of about twelve was checking into the hotel with his mother when all of a sudden he realized that he was standing next to a Beatle. He was so stunned that he turned to Paul and started pointing at him and stammering, "You're…you're… you're…you're…." "That's right," Paul interrupted, "Stevie Wonder!" "Right," the young fellow quickly agreed, "Stevie Wonder!" As we walked away, the boy's eyes and mouth remained frozen in the maxed-out open position until we walked out the door and into the garden paths that led to the bungalow outside the lobby.

Interestingly, Paul would always have this startled look on his face at the public's response when we got out of a limo or walked into a restaurant. He would act genuinely amazed at the reaction of people to his presence. His worldwide fame at that time was about four years old, and it was all so out of whack with his upbringing that he still couldn't get a grasp on it. He would shake his head and say to me, "I just don't understand."

Also, this trip was different for Paul—traveling alone at times without entourage and all the customary hype. Although Ron Kass, Tony Bramwell, and Paul's childhood friend Ivan Vaughn (the classmate who introduced Paul to John all those years earlier) accompanied Paul on this trip, they often weren't around when we made the various personal and promotional rounds. Especially in the United States, Paul was not used to moving around in relative secrecy. This solo flight (that is, without the other Beatles) allowed him to see things from a different perspective. He commented one night in the hotel suite that for so long the Beatles had had to enter buildings, restaurants, hotels, and the like by service entrances, basement tunnels, alley doors, etc., that it was nice to see the front entrances and nice parts of the places he was visiting on this U.S. visit. American hotel lobbies and curbsides were new to him.

OB-LA-DI, OB-LA-DA

The next day, I was hanging about the bungalow, being generally available, while Paul was writing new songs and rewriting others. Ron Kass had tried to convince Paul to carry a tape recorder of some sort around with him because Paul would write incredible song after incredible song and then totally forget them. He would sing an absolute stunner to us in the living room on Monday, and then on Tuesday we would ask him to sing that great song he wrote the day before, and he wouldn't have a clue what we were talking about. Anyway, because I was there, hanging about, he started including me in his musical constructions. I got wrapped up that afternoon in the words and intent of "Ob-La-Di, Ob-La-Da" and "Back in the USSR." On the way home that night, I realized I had, in a sense, just spent the afternoon songwriting with Paul McCartney! Of course, when the album came out later, I wasn't surprised when I didn't see my name as a cowriter.

I was surprised, however, to see the songs listed as Lennon- McCartney compositions, because to my knowledge, John had nothing to do with them. That's when I learned something. Although the public was still mostly unaware of the unique nature of the world-famous Lennon-McCartney songwriting team, I began to vaguely grasp the unspoken part of the intangible structure of their business, as well as their musical and personal friendship. They told me that they considered each other, at that time, such an integral part of each other's influences that they were in some ethereal way writing songs together, even when apart. For me, it was a unique day that didn't necessarily pay well but was one that money can't buy (me luv). To this day, I wouldn't trade it for anything.

GOT TO GET YOU INTO MY LIFE

That day had an unusual ending. We had taken a break, and Paul had gone into the bathroom. The suite was laid out with a dining area and living area on one side separated by a hall that ran alongside with a bedroom at each end and a bath-room in the middle. The door to the hallway was midway between the dining and living areas. With Paul out of the room, I answered a knock at the door and met Linda Eastman for the first time. "Hello, may I help you?" I asked. Speaking through me, not to me, she vaguely replied, "Is Paul here?" Over my shoulder, she saw Paul coming through the door that led from the bedroom/bathroom portion of the suite and wham— she went past me like a Notre Dame football tackle. She full force embraced him in the doorway, push-pulled him through it, slammed it shut, and that was the last I saw of him or her that day.

I waited around for about an hour because I had this great idea for a line in "Ob-La-Di, Ob-La-Da" that I knew he was dying to hear. I finally gave up and went home. I am not quite sure what happened that night, but I do know that Linda was with us until I put them on a plane heading east (man!).

LINDA IN THE SKY WITH....

The next day, I drove Paul and Linda to LAX. They were flying to New York together and then he was going ahead on to London. After we had checked in and secured tickets and seating arrangements, Paul announced that he was hungry and opted for a hot dog from a little stand LAX used to have at the top of the escalators. These stands were short-lived but were strategically placed close to the gates so that people in a hurry could grab a quick bite to eat. We went to the stand, ordered a couple of dogs, and stood at the stand and ate them. Paul McCartney caused bedlam wherever he went, yet that day, no one was even aware that they were standing elbow to elbow with a Beatle while they were grabbing their fast eats.

Ken and Paul "in step" as they leave a Hollywood restaurant after a full-blown Polynesian food fest.

We started back toward the gate when we were gathered up by a group of airport officials who advised us that there was a bomb threat on the plane. They explained that they had set aside a special room for our comfort so that Paul wouldn't be mobbed by the crowds during an extended wait. The wait did become extended, and a couple of hours soon passed. I later found out that the bomb scare was a ruse—they were actually going through Paul's luggage searching for drugs! (Years later I went through a horrendous experience with Pattie Harrison when she was given a "complete" body search for the same reason at this same airport.)

The airport officials found no bomb (or drugs!), and it was finally time to board. During the long wait, we had talked about England, and I told him how much I was looking forward to my first trip to London. (I had not yet been officially appointed to the Apple U.S. manager position and at that time was acting in the capacity of Capitol's national promotion manager and director of the Artist Relations Department. I didn't know how involved I would be with the Apple venture.) Before leaving, Paul took a medallion he had worn during the trip from around his neck and put it around mine. I had admired it earlier in the week because of its uniqueness. "You better be wearing this the next time I see you," he said. He started boarding, stopped, turned around, and said, "In London!"

As it turned out, Ron Kass told me later that McCartney was mainly responsible for bringing me to Apple and had already made the decision when he left L.A. that day.

Those were the days, my friend, but that was *the* day as far as I am concerned!

Beauty and the Beach

JANUARY 1994
TWENTY-SIX YEARS LATER

Bodega Bay, California

The tides this winter are higher than they have ever been before here on this magnificent northern California coastline. Anyway, that is what some of the locals say. When it comes to regional facts such as these, their manner and presentation of information has such a tone of indisputable authenticity that I accept it as a legally documentable and historical statistic:

The tides this winter on the northern California coast have never been this high before! So be it!

The waves have washed the entire beach clean of debris. Caught up in an aggressive land attack, they even surge up through the seaside grasses that cling to the dunes above the shore. This watery intrusion leaves the beach looking like it has been scrubbed and shaved. The grasses lay flat as if they have just had a cosmic shampoo. This prepped look coupled with the brilliance of the winter sun and the turbulent surf gives my morning walk a vibrancy and edge I have never experienced before. With every new weather wonder and seasonal surprise, I am thrown deeper into praise and amazement at the glory of a most powerful and omniscient heavenly Father.

As I walk today on the small portion of the sand left for me by the tide, I am caught up in perception of having a problem with my walk. Because the tide line forces me up into the soft sand at the foot of the dunes, it is hard to find firm footing. Because I am having trouble focusing on my relationship with God, my spiritual walk also feels like I am walking in shifting sand instead of on the rock foundation Christ has laid out for me. I am so used to trials and rough circumstances that I am having trouble enjoying this exhilarating aspect of my covenant. I am completely filled with praise to my merciful and loving Creator for placing me in this beautiful place—yet I gaze out to sea in disbelief and begin to feel guilty.

I guess I actually miss the closeness I experience when my pain is overwhelming. I miss crying out to him and pleading with him to bend down and touch me with his merciful and healing hands. I love hearing his blessed assurance when all seems lost. Nothing is more beautiful than sensing his arms around my very being during these trying times. They let me know he is God and I am his. I am reassured that all things that happen are in accordance with his divine plan. Deep inside, I know everything will be all right if I will just trust in him.

At times like these, he has a way with me through the absolute simplicity and clarity of his Word. If he were to write me a letter in answer to my questionings, I imagine it would read something like this:

GOD

Eternity

God the Father
C.E.O.
Heaven

Dear Ken:

Either you believe or you don't.

Love,
God the Father

cc: Jesus, the Holy Spirit, the Saints

He tells me that if I believe we must suffer at times without explanation, then I also have to believe him when he promises undeserved blessings. If I believe in humility and contrition, then I must also believe that he delights in giving us our hearts' desires. If I believe that I am to give the shirt from my back to my fellowman, then I must believe that I will drink the fine wines from vineyards I didn't plant. He did not give us his Word to pick and choose only the parts that work for us or condemn us. Also he does not suggest that we should go on a "bummer" and live out solely what we perceive as bad news. After all, he is the God of the Good

News! In fact, he asks us in his Word to see him not as a God of wrath but as a God of grace and blessing!

I was a devoted follower (and subsequently one of its leaders) of the metaphysical religious movement in the 1960s and 1970s, which was great—for a while. These were take-one-from-column-A-and- two-from-column-B religions. If I didn't believe in sexual purity or that there was anything wrong with doing drugs, for instance, then I could just incorporate a sympathetic teaching into my do-it yourself path of many paths up the mountain of holiness. It was easy to be spiritual when you didn't really have to change anything about yourself! All you had to do was adapt elliptical, ethereal descriptions of both your vices and good points into one cohesive concept, pick a mantra, sit in funny positions, smile when you were insulted, bless those who didn't quite understand, and automatically you and God were pals. In retrospect, I find it was more a matter of semantics than religion. Presentation and perception were immensely more important than ideals.

I love being a Christian. I love the Bible, God's holy Word, and believe that he is the almighty Creator of all things and in total control of all things at all times. I also believe that the Holy Bible's form and content are exactly as he intended for my eyes and heart at this time and in this place. If he wanted even a single word of the Book I hold in my hands to be different for my understanding, then I am sure he would supernaturally change it when I wasn't looking.

Either I believe or I don't! I believe that he is perfect and makes no mistakes. I believe every word he says. I believe that it is not necessary for me to understand a lot or a little. Comprehension is not a requirement of my salvation. Faith is!

I love it in the Bible when Job repented after questioning God and cried, "I am nothing—how could I ever find the answers? I lay my hand upon my mouth in silence. I have said too much already" (Job 40:4–5). How can we even think in our wildest dreams that we can understand his ways in our present state? He promises great revelation some day, and that is good enough for me. I am so happy that he is in charge. I feel so much better now that I have given him permission to go ahead and take charge of my affairs. I bet that he was relieved when I finally agreed to let him have his way with me!

I awaken from these rambling thoughts about my loving heavenly Father to the sound of almost twenty-foot surf crashing in upon itself only a hundred feet from the shore. It crashes downward and then sprays upward—roaring and soaring for anyone, no one, or everyone to hear. I love the crashing breakers for their bravado in this scenario. They don't really care if I or anyone else is observing, agreeing, or running to or from their presentation. They are just doing what God has set them about to do. They only have purpose—no questions asked—just forward, free, full-blown obedience to what they were intended. Oh how I long to fall in line with God's purpose for me with this same incredible exuberance as I, too, come crashing daily upon these shores. How can you question obedience like the constant waves— a love that expresses itself when no one's watching!

I wrap the wind around me. I soothe my soul with the shimmering sun. I blend with the beach and talk to the terns. I walk with the waves and bathe in the blessings of God's greatness.

I am secure in his love because I believe him.

By the will he has given me, I choose to believe every word he says is true.

I fall—he catches. I stagger—he straightens. I falter—he smoothes the way. He is love—I am a partaker. I question—he answers. Because he is all—I need nothing. I fall to my knees in the sand—he is around me—in me—before me—for me. Yes, I am blessed among men. There is incredible beauty on this beach. The driftwood here was hand-hewn by the gentle carpenter himself. I bow my head—he lifts my spirit. I see the sea—he sees me and forgives, forgets, heals, and binds the wounds of my wickedness.

"I stand before Him convicted, confessing that most of my wounds have been self-inflicted."[2]

He weeps for me like he wept for Lazarus (John 11:35)—out of compassion and love. He knows my sin is killing me. He defends me against worldly persecution like he did the adulterous woman facing the stones of hypocrisy (John 8:1–11; Luke 19:1–8). He grants me revelation before the waters of this ocean like he did the woman before the waters of the well (John 4:14). He begs me to come down from the trees of my haughtiness like he did Zacchaeus so he can stay with me, sup with me, and draw me into his way and his purpose (Luke 19:1–10). He washes my feet with his humility and then teaches me how to walk (John 13:1– 17). He turns the tables in the temples of my transgressions. He leads me to eternal peace—if I will just follow.

He is my friend, my teacher, my healer, and my Savior. He is the beauty on this beach. He is the beauty in my life. I am privileged to gaze into the eyes of this Man of sorrows and hold onto his nail-scarred hands.

He died for me, so I must—I absolutely must—live for him in return.

---

2 Lyric from a song written by Nashville Christian songwriter Gary Dunham.

He gives power to the tired and worn out, and strength to the weak. Even the youths shall be exhausted, and the young men will all give up. But they that wait upon the Lord shall renew their strength. They shall mount up with wings like eagles; they shall run and not be weary; they shall walk and not faint.

ISAIAH 40:29-31

Hello, Goodbye

JULY 1968
TWENTY-SIX YEARS EARLIER

London, England

Knock knock. "Hello, my name is Peter Brown, and I am the chief of protocol for the Beatles, and I have come to give you your 'shedjule' [schedule]." He then continued on officiously with outlining the said "shedjule" without any response from me or even a little transitory chitchat. His approach was proper; clear of purpose; and "veddy, veddy" (very, very) English. There was no question that we would be spending quite a lot of time communicating with each other over the months or years ahead, but right now he had an agenda, and we were going to discuss my "shedjule."

LONDON ARRIVAL

I was still in somewhat of a daze. Peter Asher met our plane at Heathrow, and after he and I had our mini reunion, which included my inquiry into the well-being and whereabouts of my friend and his ex-partner, Gordon Waller, Peter adeptly ushered us curbside at Heathrow and presented us with our uniformed chauffeur, who snapped us a curt salute as he held forth stiffly in front of our personal white Rolls

JULY 1968

Recording sessions for the White Album are in full bloom. Many songs are completed or are in various stages of completion, including "Everybody's Got Something to Hide Except me and my Monkey," "Ob-La-Di, Ob La Da," "Revolution," Sexy Sadie," "Don't Pass me By," While My Guitar Gently Weeps" and "Hey Jude."

Paul McCartney's long-term girlfriend Jane Asher announces in a BBC television interview that her engagement to Paul is off.

All four Beatles attend the world premiere of the animated Yellow Submarine *film at the London Pavilion.*

Royce limousine. Apple had graciously provided us this classy perk on a twenty-four-hour basis for the entire visit. We were then driven (without our baggage, because naturally someone would see that it was properly delivered) to our waiting suites at an exclusive Hyde Park hotel. Of course we were preregistered, pre-checked in, prima donna'd in every way.

It was special being with Peter again. We had become good friends during the "Peter and Gordon" visits to California, where my responsibility as head of promotion and artist relations was to spend the entire time with them during their visits and tours. I would meet them at the airport in Los Angeles and cart them off to their hotel. Now, he had just met me at the airport and had just delivered me to my hotel. There was a continuous irony in our relationship in that after Peter and Gordon and our Capitol Records stint, Peter and I ended up at Apple. We next became vice presidents at MGM together, which was followed by our both leaving the loony lion to eventually become independent record producers. To give this sequence of events a perpetual feel, as record producers we both scored chart-topping singles at the same time with similar artists (Linda Ronstadt and Jessi Colter). Coincidentally, but not surprisingly, we then found ourselves mixing our competitive hit albums side by side in the same town (Hollywood) at the same studio (the Sound Factory) for the same record label (Capitol).

Anyway, I was still looking out the window at my beautiful view of the park and listening to the stereo system and complete selection of current English rock albums libraried in my room by the Beatles' personal staff when Peter Brown came to my door.

"…We will begin with tea at 3 Savile Row [catered by Fortnum and Mason], next you will be having lunch with all four of the lads [and Yoko] at the Ritz Hotel in Piccadilly to get better acquainted, and then we will go directly into meetings for the rest of the day," he continued. "At approximately 17:00 hours, you will be returned to your suite and allowed time to freshen up. Tonight, Ringo will be taking you to dinner and then to the theater to see the new Robert Morely play, *Halfway up the Tree*, written by Peter Ustinov and directed by John Gielgud. Tomorrow morning, you will have breakfast with George. Afterwards, it's back into meetings, and then you'll be having lunch with all four of the lads in the private restaurant on top of the hotel that has been reserved for just our group. We will continue meetings for the afternoon, and then Paul will take you nightclubbing that evening." Peter Brown clearly laid out our whole itinerary for the entire visit—a perfect blend of subtly tourist things and hip insider jaunts that would help meld us into the organization. There was the obvious proper mixture of being with all four Beatles as well as one-on-one time spent in various activities.

I liked Peter Brown a lot upon this first meeting. He reminded me of a regal-rock-and-proper-roll version of Peter Ustinov. I later learned that his high-hat, upper-class British snobbery had only recently replaced a common upbringing akin to the other members of the Apple corps. As a supporting cast member of this unfolding play on words and music, he definitely was an Academy Award winner. I was very disappointed in the slant he took in his book *The Love You Make*. After reading it, I look back now and, in retro-observation, feel that in terms of Peter Brown, *act* was the operative word when referring to him as a "class act." I was in the room during different instances he wrote about in his book, so I found it odd that he named everyone there except me. Although I must confess that my ego was a little miffed, historically because of this discrepancy I found I greatly questioned the other stories in his book where I wasn't present. My greatest objection was to the dark-side approach he took to events and the Beatles themselves. I think there must have been two John Lennons—I never met his!

The chauffeur became a regular member of our visit, and as protocol dictated, he never spoke to us first; he only responded when a conversation was initiated on our part. His answers were to the point and always courteous. If he did need to make an unsponsored comment (like if my hair was on fire or something), he always asked permission to speak before actually doing so—if that's possible! We sometimes kept him going for twenty-four hours in a row, and he was always crisp, polite, alert, and available to our service at all times—no complaints, just proper demeanor and courtesy.

THE APPLE MEETINGS

One would think that trying to schedule and hold formal meetings with the members of a successful four-piece rock and roll band would be like trying to organize fire ants into straight columns, but it was quite the opposite with the Beatles. They had accomplished about everything there was in the category of rock stars, and they took the Apple endeavor very seriously. I wish some of my other business associates over the years could have been as punctual and attentive to the matters at hand—and as enthusiastic! Their fame and fortune allowed them to play businessmen! But like Joe Montana when he played football, they were not playing around. They really enjoyed this new career in the beginning and were truly into it on all levels. As crazy as the whole thing was, I defy any other group of this stature to be as focused and coordinated in effort and spirit as this one was at the outset.

Apple was fun. Apple had heart and a philosophy of good intent. It had good people and good music. Good Lord, I wish it could have lasted.

A large suite had been reserved for the week in Hyde Park's Royal Lancaster Hotel, and that is where we met. The days were Long, and we worked hard. We would break for lunch in the showroom on the top floor that was only open in the evenings. The room was a classic English supper club that featured dining and dancing to a four-piece band. We were served our noon meal there without the obvious intrusion of fans during these needed breaks.

One day, Stan, Larry, a few Apple staffers, and I got a surprise musical treat. We were seated at a ringside table in front of the bandstand, and as we were finishing lunch, Paul got up, sat down behind the drum kit, and started laying down a pattern on the drums. Before long, all four Beatles were onstage jamming on instruments other than the ones they were noted for. They played a twenty-minute impromptu set for us—their delighted guests. Musicians sure do like music!

Pickers sure do like to pick! We sure did enjoy watching and listening to our employers at work!

During the nonmusical portion of these meetings, we decided on a six-man promotion team that I would set up on a regional basis when I returned to the United States. This team would be drawn from the elite of Capitol's fifty-man field team that I had put together over the years. I knew every man well and had hired most of them personally. Gortikov approved this team as a Capitol expenditure and felt that the other six or seven small independent labels that I was responsible for could use this promotional "swat team's" efforts as well. We decided on the first four releases,[3] mapped out the original release campaign, and decided it would culminate in the "Golden Apple" award[4] ceremony to be held in L.A. at the then "happening" Sunset Strip Playboy Club. The Playboy Club—times have changed!

Probably the most memorable part of these meetings was Paul's personal dilemma over the first Beatle release to be included in the "First Four." Although the "a" and "b" songs had been selected— "Hey Jude" and "Revolution"—Paul had serious misgivings about the acceptability of "Hey Jude's"

---

3 The first four records to be released on Apple Records were: the Beatles' "Hey Jude" backed with "Revolution"; Mary Hopkin's "Those Were the Days" backed with "Turn, Turn, Turn"; Jackie Lomax's "Sour Milk Sea" backed with "The Eagle Laughs at You"; and the Black Dyke Mills Band's "Thingumybob" backed with "Yellow Submarine." The advertising agency of Wolfe and Ollins designed the "Our First Four" plastic 10-by-12-inch black matte box that encased hand-lathed versions of these records with handwritten labels by the Beatles. The outside top lid said "Our First Four," 3 Savile Row, with Stanley Gortikov, Larry Delaney, and Ken Mansfield individually listed on the front. This special package also contained photos and bios along with the records.

4 The basic concept of the competition between Capitol's field promotion staff for this award was based on setting a formula for airplay and sales on a territorial basis. The promotion man who got the most airplay on designated key stations and caused the most sales on the first four Apple releases would be flown first class to L.A. There, he would be rewarded with a banquet in his honor and presented a large beautiful golden Apple as a trophy. The "icing on the cake" was that one of the Beatles would fly in from London and present the trophy to the contest winner in person. The fact that the L.A. guy won the award and the banquet was coincidentally planned while George Harrison was in town on other business had nothing to do with the time, place, and date of this glamorous event!

length. We adjourned to the new Apple building on 3 Savile Row where a professional tape deck and giant sound system had been set up in one of the large rooms. At that point, the building had been carpeted with dark green carpet and painted inside and out in white. There was no other furniture or accouterments except a table set with refreshments and snacks at the opposite end of the same room. We sat on the floor for extended periods of time playing the two songs over and over, trying to decide which one to release as the "A-side." We were playing by the rules that said all new releases had the "A-side" or "B-side" designated for Top 40 airplay purposes. The mechanical reason for this was so that when a record company released an artist's new record, the promotion men would all push the same song for airplay in order to create a hit song. In other words, if 100 percent of the important radio stations played one side of a record, you had a hit. If 50 percent of the stations played one side and 50 percent played the other side, you had a mediocre chance at success. The irony of this dilemma was that every station played every song the Beatles released. They were going to play both sides anyway, but Paul wanted to do it by the numbers.

It was amazing to sit on the floor in front of the speakers and witness Paul's artistic insecurity. Somehow, fear of rejection didn't seem an appropriate emotion in that room! (Looking back, one thing I find great joy in is the fact that I don't ever remember any of the Beatles suggesting that one solution to this problem would be to shorten the record.)

It seemed the playbacks would go on forever, until I came up with a suggestion that put Paul at ease. I volunteered to reroute myself on the way back to L.A. via a few key airplay markets if he would trust me with one advance copy of the record. I would hopscotch my way to Philadelphia and play it for Jim Hilliard at WFIL, then continue on to Jim Dunlap at WQAM in Miami, etc. These men and a few others at American Top 40 stations at that time were known and respected for their ability to "pick the hits." Then when I got back to L.A., I would call Paul and let him know the results. He liked the idea. I really liked the idea, because not only was it a very neat first assignment, but it was a great PR move for me with some major radio stations. Needless to say, the music directors fell out of their trees when they heard "Hey Jude." Such a hesitant start to possibly the Beatles' greatest record!

At the conclusion of the hotel meetings and the signing of the Apple contracts by Gortikov and the four Beatles, they presented Stan, Larry, and me with hand-lathed 45rpm copies of the first four records. The labels were handwritten by the Beatles themselves. They had packaged them in black plastic boxes with our names, a green Apple, and "First Four" embossed on the front. (Many years later, in Nashville, I had to decide between eating and looking at that package. This unique treasured gift from the Beatles represented a time in my life in which I felt very alive and vital. In Tennessee, I had to sell it for "vittles" to stay alive.) Stanley had arranged to present them with a special crystal Apple that didn't make it to the meetings, so he symbolically presented them with a real apple instead. On the table with the documents, the real apple had been placed in the center. After the contracts were signed, Paul picked up the apple, walked away from the others, and ate it.

Years later, after the breakup, I was rummaging through some old boxes in my closet and out fell this picture of Paul standing apart from the others—back turned to them, staring out the window and finishing off the apple. The symbolism and foreshadowing inherent in that action rushed over me like a giant emotional tidal wave. It also made me wonder how often and how far back in our lives we are given metaphoric information of things that will someday happen.

I've included the picture here—I don't think any of the Beatles have ever seen it.

The signing of the Apple contracts giving Capitol the rights to distribute Apple Records and the agreement that the Beatles could release future product on Apple Records. Paul stands separate from the others eating the apple—a foretelling?

Victory at Sea

APRIL 1996
TWENTY-EIGHT YEARS LATER

Bodega Bay, California

In the outer middle of Bodega Bay Harbor stands a small rock island the locals call Bird Rock, Bodega Rock, and even Seal Rock. It always draws your attention as you stare out across the bay, the harbor, and the vast Pacific Ocean beyond. It is a refuge for harbor seals, a multitude of birds, and beneath the tide lines various mussels, abalone, etc., cling for their brief dear lives.

When I was young, I would attempt to swim out to a rock such as this and either accomplish the feat or survive in some youthful victorious way. In those evenings, we would dance around the fires, walk through the waves, run ahead of the wind, and claim the shore and all that it held for us. We had an energy that virtually supersurged through us, always escaping and emerging in the free form of our indestructibility, our passion, our laughter, our dreams, and our unending conquests of either whatever caught our attention or got in our way. This is what we did in our teens and twenties.

As time passed, our enthusiasm became checkered with limiting realities, but that fire within would keep reigniting.

Needing only the slightest hope of victory, it would fan alive and burn bright again, ready to light up new worlds and burn old bridges. This was known as the journey through our thirties! As our forties frantically dwindled away, the bonfires took longer to build, were harder to light, burned dimmer, and had fewer people dancing around them. Much to our ego-laden surprise, many of us suddenly realized that we had been left to clean up the ashes by ourselves. By the time we stumbled into our fifties, dazed and confused, we found ourselves just trying to keep warm and relevant, close to home—wildfires replaced with home fires and heating pads![5]

I can hear the harbor seals barking from the rock like big lonely dogs when I walk on the beach every morning. Sometimes I can't see the rock because of the mist or fog, but I know it's there. I realize that even though I can't see it and have never touched it, it sustains life because it is immovable, solid, and unchanging. I love the way God speaks to me—not in audible words but in thoughts that appear from the mist, or should I say from the mystery. He guided my thoughts to the rock and told me that he is the Rock and that I have been trying to carry the rock on my shoulders instead of standing on the Rock. He said I should depend on the Rock, trust the Rock like the seals and birds place their trust on the rock for life, sustenance, and refuge from the storm. He said I should try standing on the Rock, that I would be surprised how much clearer the view was from there, how differently things look from his perspective, and how peaceful it can be to rest there. Like the rock in Bodega Bay, I could be washed clean by the waves of his Word washing over me every day.

---

5   By the way, as for how we feel in our sixties—see the part about our teens and twenties!

I suddenly realize that ever since the 1950s there has been "rock" in my life. As time and circumstances have evolved, always pushing me to some edge, I now find myself standing on this edge of the world, spending more time in contemplation of the Rock. The pulse and beat of the rock, rocks, and rockings of my past are being drowned out by the waves and the soft sweet rhythmic roll of his merciful love in my heart of hearts.

As I walk away from the beach toward the house, I turn back and see a father and son riding horses down the beach, racing the wind to the end of the dawn. I look past their motion at the rock in the distance and begin wondering if the seals are barking or praying. I decide to join them in giving thanks for his steadfast love and this safe harbor.

Even strong young lions sometimes go hungry, but those of us who reverence the Lord will never lack any good thing.

PSALM 34:10

Up on the Roof

JANUARY 30, 1969
TWENTY-SEVEN YEARS EARLIER

3 Savile Row

f I had to single out one event that stood out above all the others during the time I worked with the Beatles, it would by far be their last concert. It presented the end of a time warp, an intimate gathering, a worldwide event. I'm referring to their concert on the roof of Apple Records during the cold midday of Thursday, January 30, 1969. The fact that I ended up becoming a small part of the historical musical phenomenon called the Beatles began with being in the right place at the right time. The fact that I was working at Apple in London when this event took place is probably the penultimate example of this good fortune in my entertainment business life.

The *Let It Be* recordings, (which were called *Get Back* at that stage) were wrapping up, and we still hadn't accomplished the live footage segment that was planned for the movie. Apple executive Jack Oliver, who was the head of the production department and the foreign department, told me that they had tried to schedule a club in Germany by booking the Beatles under a different name: Ricky and the Red Streaks. The idea was to sneak the lads in, and when the local patrons showed up at this small club to see this new group from England, they would get the surprise of their lives when the Beatles walked out on stage and did an "à la Cavern" show. This club gig would be filmed for footage in the *Let It Be* film. Of course this was a great idea, but as you can imagine, it was in reality an unkeepable secret. Word would always get out before the show date and the usual mania madness would begin.

Then came the craziest and most short-lived idea for a concert: Mal and I had the brief assignment of scouting out deserts for a giant one-time, free Beatles concert. Mal was to check some African deserts, and I was to look at locations in our southwestern United States. The idea was to set up in the middle of nowhere, announce a date, and then invite anyone and everyone who wanted to, to come see the Beatles perform live—for free!

It didn't take long to realize that the logistics and realities of this idea were preposterous, to say the least. First of all, every kid in the world would trek to this location, and the mass numbers would be overwhelming. Forget about staging, sound systems, accommodations, travel, etc. It was the stark reality of not enough toilets that killed this idea. Besides, who was going to pay for all this? How would you like to look for an insurance underwriter for this Fab Four fiasco? We figured only about half the people would return alive from this adventure. It would end up being every concert nightmare rolled up into one and then multiplied to the tenth power. The Rolling Stones' Altamont concert would look like a prayer meeting in comparison.

The Beatles had a frustrating problem. They were a performing, live-in-your-face rock and roll band. Their immense fame swept them up and away from the very thing they did best and loved the most—rocking out in the purest rock and roll sense to a breathing, sweating live audience with the front row only a few feet away. I remember conversations that addressed this performance issue all the way back to the original Apple meetings. They were in the awkward position of suffering from their own colossal celebrity. John expressed it best when he said that "people have built us up so big in their minds that there is no way that we could go out on stage and live up to their expectations." *Sgt. Pepper* only made matters worse. A formal "live" concert tour was out of the question, no matter how many times it was brought up, but the need and a desire for a live show was still there.

The roof was a last minute and logical answer to getting live footage for the film. Apple staffers, stage crews, and carpenters readied the roof surface as well as the video and recording electronics. It was an actual gig. There was a time, a place, and a band. There was no advance publicity, but we definitely ended up with an audience. As zero hour neared (I think it was Mal who locked the downstairs doors), staffers, stagers, and stars alike all became willing prisoners of love of history and music that wonderful day at 3 Savile Row.

You had to be in London during the summer of 1969, that sun-dizzy, joss-scented season when the '60s truly seemed as if they could swing on forever. Back then, London's most talked about building was not Buckingham Palace or Parliament; it was the Georgian house on Savile Row that the Beatles had made the headquarters of their business empire, Apple Corps.

PHILIP NORMAN ON
DEREK TAYLOR'S DEATH.
ROLLING STONE,
OCTOBER 30, 1997

Ken (in the white trench coat) huddles from the cold against the chimney between Yoko, Maureen Starkey and Apple staffer Chris O'Dell, while the Beatles perform "live" for the last time for an audience of about twelve lucky souls.

What a sense of calm mixed with anticipation once the doors were locked and there was no doubt that it was a go. We were kids playing with things bigger than we understood. On the roof, howeverz, it was just us, and it felt good. It was personal; it was special, a gathering of rock and roll angels expecting to fly. Words and music would soon soar out of the very heart of the staid financial district and into the ears and souls of the unexpecting people on the streets.

London was the center of cutting-edge music, and in the neighboring buildings of this vibrant city, secretaries, bankers, and deliverymen alike were jolted alive by some magnificent men making Mersey memoric music in Mecca! Everyone within a mile of that place that day will proudly state for the rest of their lives that they were there the day the music came wafting down the streets, echoing and slamming up against the red brick buildings. Melodies and rim shots blew in through the cracks and into board meetings, while lords and loonies alike stood frozen up and down the row, blended and surrealized, side by side, necks craned upward to the rooftops. They knew immediately who it was—they were just trying to figure out how it was happening. These were not the usual sounds coming down the roads of London's financial district at lunchtime.

Soon the streets and sidewalks were clogged by voluntary standstill, open windows started dotting the sides of the once-sealed buildings, and bodies started lining the ledges of the adjoining structures. It was all unexplainable yet incredibly wonderful.

For a while I stood a few feet from George with four lit cigarettes between my fingers so he could reach over and warm the tips of his fingers. Chris O'Dell (Peter Asher's assistant), Yoko Ono, Maureen Starkey, and I huddled together against the smokestack on the roof for warmth. My unlined light beige raincoat became frozen stiff and offered little protection from the cold. By this time, I was a total Southern Californian who hadn't experienced a real winter in many years and hated it when the weather started dipping down into the low fifties, but you could have hosed me down in my shorts with ice water and I wouldn't have left this "happening" on the roof for all the money in the world!

If you ever want to find out just how good the Beatles were as a single-unit, live, four-piece, rock and roll band, just listen to the live recordings of the concert on the roof that day. Almost every conceivable obstacle was set before them. This was a band who hadn't done a live show since August 29, 1966, at San Francisco's Candlestick Park. Then there were the pressures of the Apple empire. This group of still-idealist young men were dealing with some very heavy internal business problems and dissension that touched each of them deeply. They also had a deadline. And did I mention that it was windy, damp, and frighteningly cold up on that roof that day? But just listen to how well they played and sang under those conditions. After thirty years in the heart of the record business—offstage, onstage, and backstage with everyone from Roy Orbison to Don Ho—I personally feel that the Beatles were the greatest rock and roll band of all time. Their fame wasn't a Milli Vanilli happenstance. They made it because, as Ringo simply mused, "We were a good band."

* * * *

Although this was undeniably the biggest event in my entertainment career, it is perhaps the smallest event inside this day that I remember the most. We had set a "lunchtime" showtime, and the Beatles all showed up in time to be onstage at that time. I walked into the office they were using as a dressing room to give a message to John; what I saw was a young group of rockers going over their set and showing signs of nervousness and pre-stage jitters just like any other band.

Suddenly it was time. They came out of the makeshift dressing room, through the door, and onto the roof stage just as I had seen other bands do a thousand times. I witnessed that unique moment for entertainers when they are told "It's time" and they journey that strange distance from the dressing room out onto the stage. Until they know they've connected with the audience, there is a deep-down, indescribable fear of not pulling it off, no matter who you are. (Andy Williams told me that even after decades of super success and thousands of concerts, he still wants to throw up just before going onstage.) Football players say they experience similar feelings until they have their first physical hit on the field—at that point, they are finally in the game.

The rules to this game had changed somewhere along the way. Confused and unamused, the players decided to play just one more time—a whole note…a final chord.

The Beatles burst through the door to the stage and did their last concert.

When it was over, I wanted more. I still do.

There never were, and never will be, any encores.

Without Using Your Hands

JUNE 1994
TWENTY-FIVE YEARS LATER

Bodega Bay, California

graduated from a southern California coastal town college—San Diego State (or as it was better known by our rivals—"Tijuana Tech"!). I believe it was there that the knot that ties me to the Pacific Ocean was drawn, tightened, and firmly cinched deep into my being.

Joke fads will always be with us and even in some cases, like a song, will be retro indicators of periods in our lives. A collegiate joke structure in vogue at one time during my "manzanita" matriculation was: "How do you drive a(n) [insert ethnic group here] crazy?" The one for the Italians was: "Do you know how to drive an Italian crazy? Just say 'Can you describe how to play a trombone in a phone booth—without using your hands?'!"

What reminded me today of that particular genre of jokes was the idea of trying to walk along this shore without thinking of God! I see him in every aspect of the beauty that stretches out before me.

As I walked along the beach this morning, I believe I experienced what is probably the most beautiful day I have ever seen in my life. (My wife says I say that very thing every time I come up from the shore after my walk and talk with the magnificent Creator of all that lies before me.) Anyway, if the word spectacular has a superlative form, then that could barely describe the beauty of the bay and the heavenly harbor this morning.

As I looked out to sea, he was there just beyond the horizon. The gentle waves lapping at my feet assured me that, no matter how far away he sometimes appears to be, he is at the very point of my walk at all times. He abides deep in the waters before me, reminding me of the vastness of his love. In the quiet, he unfolds a story, the one his Son told at the well. A story about other waters—living waters. I stop as his presence overtakes me, and I turn to the tides and experience his relentless tugging at my soul. I cast my eyes downward and, in the Spirit, see between the grains of sand, believing that he truly does know each one. I know these things because he said so, and I believe every word he says. He is truth. He is perfect. He makes no mistakes. Now and always, everything will be just as he decides and as he intended. How incredible to have a God like that!

I look heavenward and think of another who also loved to walk by the sea, a young man who was the very gift from God. The One who was sent to save us, forgive us, and grant us unconditional love, magnificent mercy, and glorious grace. He was the absolute servant of all, simply bent on preparing us for an everlasting home with God the Father Almighty.

I look down the coastline and eventually my vision stops at a point where the spray and mist from the waves cause a prismatic diffusion limiting how far I can see. Like him and his way with me, there is a limit to how far I can see into his Word. Like the lifting of the fog from the shore, he will lift the scales from my eyes and grant me revelation—all in his good time and as fits his divine purpose.

There is a fine line between "pressing in" and pushing God. I can hear a soft wind behind me rustling through the golden grasses of the dunes, and although I can't see there, I know he is there. I realize I don't need to physically see my Lord and Master in order to believe in him or trust him to watch over me. He is always there—by me, above me, around me, in me, and of me. He created me for his fellowship. I am not a toy that he will discard when he tires of me; I am the apple of his eye. If I were the only person in the world, he would still have sent his Son to die for me. He has given me royal roots and an honored heritage. If only I could see me as he sees me—if only I could see him as he would have me see him!

All I know is: I love him, and even that is not of my doing. It is his beautiful gift that he has placed deep in my very being.

How can I not love a God that would do something as glorious as that?

How can I not want to obey him with all my heart?

How can I not feel my arms raise up to him in grateful thanksgiving and wondrous worship?

How can I possibly serve him—without using my hands?!

When the clouds are heavy, the rains come down; when a tree falls, whether south or north, the die is cast, for there it lies. If you wait for perfect conditions, you will never get anything done. God's ways are as mysterious as the pathway of the wind, and as the manner in which a human spirit is infused in the little body of a baby while it is yet in its mother's womb. Keep on sowing your seed, for you never know which will grow—perhaps it all will....

Young man, it's wonderful to be young! Enjoy every minute of it! Do all you want to; take in everything, but realize that you must account to God for everything you do.

ECCLESIASTES 11:3–6, 9

There's a Place

DECEMBER 1968
TWENTY-SIX YEARS EARLIER

London, England/Copenhagen, Denmark

"Let's go to lunch—there's a place I like to go." With that, Paul McCartney stood up, slipped on a light jacket, and headed out of the Apple offices front door and out onto the street with me following behind, stumbling like a small child trying to catch up. He had a favorite pub called The Green Man (there are several by this name in London, but there was one in particular that he preferred), and that's where we were going. The pub was actually a rather long way from the Apple offices, and we had to walk right through the heart of downtown London during the busy noontime midweek crowds. It is pretty amazing that he would do this because this was in 1968, and seeing a Beatle in person was a monumental traffic-stopping event in those days.

He set a brisk yet casual pace, which made us less noticeable and helped us blend more into the hurrying crowd around us. As we forged ahead, I would glance back over my shoulder, and it was like looking at the wake behind a speedboat. The people would hurry by, never dreaming they would be bumping against a Beatle, and then suddenly it

NOVEMBER 1968

U.S. release of John and Yoko's Two Virgins *album*

would register. They would suddenly emerge from their thoughts, stop in their tracks, and then turn around and look after us in transfixed wonder.

We arrived at The Green Man, and inside and out it looked exactly like you would imagine a typical English pub: dark worn woods, people playing darts and drinking dark pints of ale. In the center was the crowded bar, with steak and kidney pie, shepherd's pie, and other rectangular heavy glass dishes and pans filled with hearty looking foods warming behind the bar.

Our arrival was rather ordinary as far as the reaction from the patrons. Most of them were regulars, as was Paul, and he was able to go there and have a fairly normal lunch. The ruddy English lady behind the bar (Annie) was right out of a Dickens novel. As soon as Paul and I sat down for lunch at the bar, she ran upstairs to her and her husband's apartment above the pub to get something from the stove that she had just cooked. Paul ordered something that sounded like "Brown and Bitters" (whatever that was) and then spun around, leaned his back against the bar, and began watching the heated dart game that had been going on behind us. There was a relaxed, natural banter going on between the bar patrons, Paul and the contestants. Compliments and friendly challenges were issued back and forth between the Beatle and the boys as they would comment on how good his music was and he would note how badly they played darts.

Annie soon returned proudly with a large steaming hot glass bowl wrapped in a blue bath towel. Through the sides of the glass I could identify potatoes, carrots, and brown things. I had long ago learned not to ask that the brown things be identified in my English pub food. I smelled it, I tasted it, and if I liked it—I ate it and let it go at that.

Annie piled our dishes high, like she was our mother, not bothering to ask what or how much we wanted for lunch. She periodically returned to examine our plates and chide Paul to eat his vegetables. We were barely finishing our meal when I began to notice how crowded it was in the pub. I turned around, and the entire place was packed beyond standing room only. Paul gave me a couple of light taps with his knee, and as if on some cue based on the tempo of his knee tap, he was up and out through the crowd, out the door, and setting a fast pace streetward back to work. I am sure this was common procedure and that he had an arrangement with Annie, because we didn't pay before leaving. Although he had warned me between bites that a speedy exit was in the works, I still had to fight my way through the crowd that quickly opened up and made way for him as he left but just as quickly closed behind him, leaving me to push my way out of the place. Again I was trying to catch up like a little kid running after his dad. By the time I was able to fall in stride with him, we were almost a block away, and the crowd, oddly enough, held back and let us disappear down the street. It seems that once we had entered the pub, the word went up and down the road outside that Paul was in The Green Man, and soon everyone crowded in to get a glimpse.

Once I had matched his pace and we were walking alone, I noticed that it was just like nothing had happened. He said that by this time, he was programmed to know about how long he had in any given place, and it was almost like anyone else hurrying through a twenty-minute lunch.

In a way, Paul still couldn't comprehend his fame; yet as time went by, he had almost unknowingly made subtle adjustments to his lifestyle to account for it. I sometimes feel as if I am telling the same story over and over when I reflect on these mini non-events, but the point is that they were such everyday straight-ahead guys that it was almost easy for me not to be in awe of them when I was working with them on a day-to-day level. They seemed so normal all the time.

We returned to the office and picked up where we left off. This particular trip had a lot to do with our conversation the day I put him on the plane in L.A. after the Capitol convention. He hadn't forgotten my comment at that time about having never been to Europe. Not only was he largely responsible for me making my first trip to London to set up the company, he also seemed to take it upon himself to see that I got over there often.

Before this meeting, I had been in Muscle Shoals, Alabama with Ric Hall working with him on his newly formed Fame record company. Fame was one of the seven other independent labels distributed by Capitol that I was responsible for in addition to Apple. During lunch, a call came in from Stanley Gortikov in Hollywood. He said Paul needed to see me in London the next day and had set up a 1:00 p.m. meeting for us at the Apple offices. I told Stanley of my artist relations concerns if I just got up and left Ric to go to another, "more important" record company, and also I was a little behind on my rest. I had been on the road for over a month without being able to find my way back home. In those days, I would get out on the road on one assignment and then crisis after crisis would arise, and I would start running from one end of the country to the other for weeks on end. Now with London on my plate (EMI's Harvest Records was also one of my eight labels), I found the daily excursion requirements stretched from Hawaii to London and all points in between. I often lost all sense of time and location.

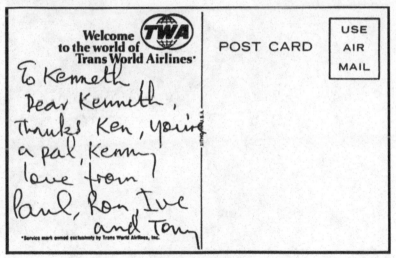

This postcard was written on a TWA flight from L.A. to London (via New York City) after Ken had taken Paul to the airport. Paul put it into an envelope and sent it regular mail from the Apple offices like a letter thus no postmark.

I also told Stan that I had no clean clothes, was out of money, and in addition to that, I didn't even know if I could get from Muscle Shoals, Alabama to London in that short time due to the limited flight schedule out of that semirural area. However, after Stan briefly reviewed (a) my responsibil-

ities, (b) the 50 percent of our business Apple factoid, and
(c) the direct relationship between my next paycheck and the
Beatles' happiness, I agreed that I could make it.

Stan said he had to go to New York the next day, so he
would have his secretary ticket him on the "red eye" and have
her book me a series of flights so I could hook up with him
at JFK. From there, I could continue straight on to London.
He said he would call my wife, have her pack for me a fresh
bag with proper clothing for that time of year in London, and
he would bring it and some cash for Europe. I was instructed

Ken and Paul face to face at an Apple meeting.

to go to the local airport immediately and then call his office to get my flight plan. This was still the 1960s, and you did have to plan your liquid cash and flight schedules a little more carefully because things weren't as automated as they are today. I also was not only changing a lot of time zones on these trips but was also jumping from climate to climate, trying to plan ahead so I would have appropriate clean clothes that could keep me both warm or cool, at least most of the time. Hotels did have valet laundry service but not when my typical schedule was to check in at midnight and checkout at 5:00 a.m. the next morning.

Getting from Muscle Shoals midday to London and Apple by 1:00 p.m. the next day with a New York City hook-up with Gortikov did take some doing. I left Ric Hall wondering "what the heck" happened to our meetings and his record company, swung by my hotel, packed and checked out in ten minutes, and continued on to the first phone booth at the airport as instructed. I called Jane at Stan's office to get my itinerary and almost immediately flew out of the Tri-City airport there—about an hour and a half after receiving the phone call from Gortikov. My first stop was Atlanta, where I changed planes for a flight to Washington D.C.'s Dulles Airport, where I again changed planes to New York City's JFK, where I had an almost Olympic relay hand-off with Gortikov as I rushed to connect with my flight to London. I slept the whole flight, jumped into a waiting car at Heathrow, checked into Claridges, and then concluded this little journey by walking into Paul's office at three minutes before 1:00 p.m., rested and wearing crisp, clean, and warm clothes over a lot of deodorant and shaving lotion. We said hi and proceeded with our meeting like I had just dropped in from across the hall.

DECEMBER 1968

Disc and Echo *magazine reports that Paul's new steady girlfriend is photographer Linda Eastman.*

World premier of film Candy, *with a cameo role by Ringo Starr.*

John and Yoko tape "Yer Blues" and an all-star jam for the Rolling Stones' "Rock and Roll Circus."

The Beatles' the White Album enters Billboard's *charts at #11, the next week hits #2, then lands in the #1 spot for nine weeks. John and Yoko appear on stage, at the Royal Albert Hall, in a white bag.*

Apple's Christmas party attended by Hell's Angels. John and Yoko appear as Father and Mother Christmas.

The content of our meeting? Paul had the artwork to Mary Hopkin's *Postcard* album spread out on his desk when I walked in. He invited me to look at it and offer my comments and observations. I said it looked good to me. He said it looked good to him too. After this brief period of review, we decided that we both felt good about it.

We were approximately 30 seconds into our 1:00 p.m. meeting at this point when Paul said that we should adjourn for now and go to our lunch at The Green Man. By the way, had I ever been to Denmark, he asked with an implied wink in his voice as I followed him out the door. He said that there's a place he wanted me to go. He wanted me to meet with the head of the EMI office in Copenhagen and get his opinion on the album cover. Paul then said that after I returned, I should probably hang out for a while around the Apple offices in case anything important came up. He said he would notify Gortikov that he needed me for a few days to help him out on the Hopkin project and a few other things!

Basically, Paul had just orchestrated a paid vacation in Europe for me. You can understand why it was hard refusing him whenever he would ask me to go out of my way for him and the others on other matters, whether Apple business or personal.

When I got off the plane in Copenhagen, the mere fact that I was there on Apple business unexpectantly garnered me special treatment. I was met by either royalty or high-ranking government officials and given the red carpet treatment for two days. Nice town. Very clean.

Peter, Appalling, & Merry

MAY 1994
TWENTY-SIX YEARS LATER

Bodega Bay, California

God is missing! I have looked for him everywhere and—he is missing! I walk and search by the water's edge. I become still before the sea. I wait...I listen and hear nothing...I cry out, and there is no answer...I cover myself by praying his very words from the Psalms—I know he cannot deny me now. He must respond. He must answer. He must speak. He must solve, repair, enhance, enable, lift, protect, give, save, solve, and solidify my situation! Why else would I have a god? Isn't he here for me and my doing? I set the stage and he does the act, right?

Can I say to you I am like Paul, Peter, Daniel, Jacob, Job, and even Esther without sounding pompous? I read of their deeds and trials and purposes and find myself lost in their love and their frustrations. In one chapter, Peter went from the man that Christ found so faithful and righteous that he called him the rock (Matthew 16:17–19) to a few verses later being the man Jesus called Satan and asked him to "get away from me" (v. 23). I realized then that Jesus loved Peter at both ends—extreme ends—saint and sinner ends—religious and sacrilegious ends—rock and brimstone ends! I realized I also fit at different times into this spectrum of obedience and faithlessness. I change and vacillate, but Jesus is always the same; he just loves me; he just hangs in there with me; he even hung on a cross for me; he is hanging in there with me now as I bounce around the walls of the upper room!

I am like the apostle Paul (Romans 7:15–17) in that I try to do what is right—I want to be obedient and pure—yet I have these thoughts; I do these things that I don't want to do; I behave in ways that are outside his purpose, outside his ways, outside his pleasure. I want to be pleasing unto him. I want to be a good and godly man, but then like a selfish fool I do the very things that he and I both don't want me to do. I go nuts with my stupidity, and he just keeps on loving me! What is wrong with this picture?

I struggle outwardly with my actions; he waits for me to settle down and bring it to him. I labor inside my reactions, and he is the calm before, after, and during the storm, always available, always ready to comfort, guide and hold me close. I wish I could love him like he loves me.

Who is missing? I go over the edge—physically, spiritually, and geographically—and he stands in place, arms outstretched, promises intact, and always available. He is perpetually moving toward me by staying steadfast in his love for me.

I often pray for great spiritual memory so I can remember his directions when trials appear. Then he answers my prayer, and I reject the Word and accept turmoil instead! He offers the peace that passes all understanding, then in my earthly nature, I pass on his peace and can't understand why my wheels keep falling off! He will guide us; he will grant us wisdom; he will protect us and provide for us in every situation! I know that!

So now I come before the Lord, Creator of all things, the Teacher of all time, the Healer of eternal things, and the ultimate Servant of all. I ask him to forgive me, hold me in his everlasting precious arms, comfort me, speak to me, guide me, grant me the simple gift of surrender so I may be pleasing unto his purpose in my life. I come to him, I bow before him, I worship him, and I plead with him.

*Lord, when you say "What do you want,"
I beseech you to heal me—if you want to!
Say to me as you said to the leper in your
Word: "Of course I want to," and then
let me be healed immediately of my iniq-
uities. Let me see the truth and be sent
out among men to speak of your almighty
power, grace, mercy, and love.*

*I love you; I praise you; I adore you and
need you above all things and desires.*

*Walk with me beside this sea like you
did with the fisherman you speak so
lovingly about.*

*Put me into the fire of Daniel and then,
because of your power and protection,
let me depart from the raging furnace
untouched by the flame.*

*Let me be like Esther when a life-and-
death task was placed before her. She
accepted peril and chose your purpose.
Like her, give me the courage to say, "If I
perish, I perish."*

*Let me prove true to you in my despair
that I trust you with the faith of Job,
and then, Almighty God, please speak
restoration into my life.*

> *If racing with mere
> men... has wearied
> you, how will you race
> against horses...? If you
> stumble and fall on open
> ground, what will you
> do in... jungles?*
>
> JEREMIAH 12:5

But like Job, I know I have said enough
already.

God isn't missing—ever!

Sometimes though—I am missing
God!

Norwegian Wood – A Separate Reality

1968-1969
TWENTY-FIVE OR
TWENTY-SIX YEARS EARLIER

3 Savile Row

I n my opinion, the only people alive today who have the right to write the Beatles' story are George, Paul, Ringo, or ex-head road manager and now Apple managing director Neil Aspinal. I honestly doubt that any of them would be moved to do so, but it still remains that they are the only ones still here and the only ones who were truly there for the duration.

There were definite insiders on various levels, of course, but anyone outside of these four people can only offer a partial, slanted, or period view at best. Because most visitors only momentarily occupied an inside position of involvement, they would be subject to the overriding rule of the woodland domain: "Unable to see the forest for the trees." I do know one thing. In those woods, it wasn't always good—like "Norwegian Wood."

I was not a full-time insider. I wasn't around in the beginning, and when I was around, I wasn't necessarily in a position of everyday confidence. But also I was not weighted down—brought to my knees—by the day-to-day intensity of the whole thing, unable to see past, through, around, or into

I am he as you are he as you are me and we are all together.

"I AM THE WALRUS"
BY JOHN LENNON AND
PAUL MCCARTNEY, 1967

things because it was all so incredibly big! As U.S. manager of Apple Records, I had my own forest to stand in—the corporate world of Capitol Records, Hollywood, where I held the additional title of director of independent labels. The Apple position placed me in the U.K., but I was only inside for days at a time by conditional circumstance or revocable personal invitations from one of the major participants. (Analogically, I considered myself an entertainment industry gardener. I had a specific job to do inside a private place, so I was allowed to witness the activity therein as long as I did my job up to their expectations. I was welcome and treated well while I was there but was expected to remain discreet when I left. The Beatles didn't write these rules; they are the rules for this business!)

I would sometimes, by default, get to briefly wear Mal Evans's hat as sidekick, because he and Neil couldn't be in four places at one time. It always amazed me how much Mal and Neil had on their plate. They seemed to be responsible for a million things, from the mundane to the intricate. Their work was personal and it was also quantitative. My observation was that they were able to pull off the impossible by making it qualitative! So little time, so many Beatles!

During George's extended visits to Los Angeles during the Jackie Lomax sessions and the re-mastering of the White Album or the completion phases of *The Concert for Bangla Desh*, I was the guy who received guests at the door, the one on the phone, the person screening the requests, and at the end of the day would be the one who rode home with the "quiet one." Life with George in these situations was always comfortable and natural, almost everyday like; he made it that way. He was easy to be with—gentle, kind, and caring. Although I was supposed to be taking care of him, he would always concern himself with how I was doing. He had a bashful, soft-spoken manner with friend and stranger alike, and he always appeared to care about others. (Years later, when I was producing Waylon Jennings, I would join the honkytonk hero on the road for a few days. I wasn't aboard for the whole tour or as a member of the band, but I traveled on the bus, in the hotel, and hung out backstage as one of the gang. I had a title [Waylon's producer] and therefore owned a validated spot inside Waylon's superstar world. But when I would begin to sense that I was starting to believe it was all real, I would—figuratively and actually—jump off the bus. After four or five days of the craziness, my internal gyroscope would start spinning out of control, and I would metaphorically emerge from the mist and seek the world for what it really was—a place without the deception of the glad-handlers, screaming crowds, and unending sensual indulgences.)

In my metaphysical days, I was a big fan of Carlos Castenada and was particularly fond of one of his most famous books, *A Separate Reality*. I would always reflect back on its central message as a lifeline I could hang on to when it became time to disconnect from the misconception of existence the road can bring. I took away from the book the simplistic interpretation that things are not always as they seem. From that, I projected into my life in the entertainment world the operational knowledge that I should never let the abstract become the front line. Real things are not real if their basis comes out of an unsubstantiated nowhere. I call it the believing-in-skyhooks syndrome. Accolades and adoration for being able to sing and whip your hips in a suggestive manner all at the same time does not make someone a master of all intelligentsia. Some of my most bizarre, clinging-to-the-edge friends were sought out for their wisdom, just because they were famous. These same people, if they broke a shoelace in the morning, were lost for the day, and yet any words that literally escaped from their numbed brains were taken as gospel truth, and lives were shaped after their insane verbiage.

The rhythm of the road and only stopping for hamburgers or living to be adored by cheering fans is not always the most intelligent approach when it comes to character building or useful information gathering. When I was out there with a famous entertainer or group, I found it was easy to get caught up in what was going on, especially when that fantasy-in-motion world began to seem like the real world. Eventually, it became hard not to believe that this separation from reality had something to do with actual life on planet Earth.

If there ever was a separate reality, I experienced it the minute I walked through the doors at 3 Savile Row—the Apple office address in London. The only thing that kept me from biting on the inviting Apple-illusion that lay therein was the mere fact that I was coming and going. I knew it would take more than a kiss to wake me up out of that dream, and fortunately, I was never there long enough to completely succumb to its altered state of rock and roll mesmerization. But I was there, both as an observer and a participant, and so I can more than imagine what it was like for the full-time staffers.

An informal meeting on the floor of the newly decorated, but unfurnished Apple office at 3 Savile Row. Clockwise from the top—Ringo, Peter Brown, George, Apple staffer, Stanley Gortikov, Larry Delaney, Ken and Peter Asher.

They spent the whole of their semi-waking hours in a Mersey-beaten vortex, pressurized by the intense focus of a socio-politically shipwrecked youth screaming to be heard above the sound of real social revolution and the deafening heartbeat of this earthshaking band.

How can persons wake up, fall out of bed, run a comb across their heads, and then work those long hours under that extreme pressure without losing touch with the reality that surrounds the dream that they "went off into"? Individually, the Beatles were incredible people. Collectively, they attracted a sterling staff—an improbable gathering of rock and roll angels who graced the core of the Apple. On a street level analytical basis, I would also like to lovingly add that the members of the Apple crew were the oddest flock of ducks I had ever met.

I walked away from that building many times, but I will never be able to leave behind the memories of those people and events.

Real or unreal—it will never happen again.

The Son
in My Eyes

MAY 1996
TWENTY-SEVEN TO
TWENTY-EIGHT YEARS LATER

Bodega Bay, California

Usually when I walk in the morning, I skirt the edge of the tideline, first heading to the north and against the wind. Actually and symbolically, this is the hard part of my walk. It is typically colder and has become the part of my morning devotion when I bow down, confess up, press in, and stress out before my heavenly Father.

Sometimes I feel I am a very part of the sea beside me—my thoughts and prayers merge into his vastness and its immensity. Today though, I feel as if the only thing I could claim in equal identification with the perpetually surging waves is that I too keep doing the same thing over and over every day. I envy the waters for their sureness of purpose. My repetitions are more in the category of hanging on to old patterns.

Suddenly I feel like I am drowning in my own confusion, still clinging to garbage long ago thrown overboard. Again and again I ride it to the dark murky bottom. My stroll has turned into a guilt trip, with Satan as my travel agent. I have left God's pathway and fallen into the chasmic itinerary of my own unacceptance of his grace and mercy. By now, my walk is going nowhere; my expectations are adrift, and my soul is tangled up in spiritual seaweed.

I turn around and turn away from these thoughts as I start walking southward with the wind and straight into the sun. Suddenly the wind at my back becomes his hand on my shoulder, and the sun on my face becomes the Son in my eyes. I stop and encounter the crashing surf head on. I walk to its edge, and the magnificence of this place once again overwhelms me. His presence engulfs me, and I begin having one of those brief rare talks with the Creator in which I actually listen and understand. His word finally touches that part deep down inside of me that harbors the child he created, and I begin weeping into the wonder of the waters he once walked on.

I look at his majesty before me, and I ask him what I have done to deserve being in this beautiful setting. He gently replies:

"Absolutely nothing!"

Then I ask what I have done that makes me totally undeserving of being here. He says:

"Absolutely everything!"

Once again my fear and doubt sail off into the Sonrise on the winds of morning grace. The sea of forgiveness beckons mercifully to another sailor lost at land.

Another Bible lesson on the beach!

The heavens are telling the glory of God; they are a marvelous display of his craftsmanship. Day and night they keep on telling about God. Without a sound or word, silent in the skies, their message reaches out to all the world. The sun lives in the heavens where God placed it and moves out across the skies as radiant as a bridegroom going to his wedding, or as joyous as an athlete looking forward to a race! The sun crosses the heavens from end to end, and nothing can hide from its heat.

PSALM 19:1-6

(Why Couldn't They Just) Let It Be

JANUARY 1969

TWENTY-SEVEN YEARS EARLIER

London, England

I had the good fortune to go to various Beatles recording sessions, which were a little different than most, to put it mildly. Even though we were among the privileged few that got to attend a Beatles session, usually we were never actually in the studio with them. The privilege of attending one of these happenings basically consisted of being invited to hang out in the halls and the lobby of the studio where they were recording. Occasionally one of them would come out on a break or hang out with us for a while. You could hear the muffled music behind the doors get loud and clear during the few seconds it would be open as they or the recording team went in and out. Still, it was an elitist event just being seen by the fans going in and out of the heavily guarded entrance to the studio. Sometimes I could feel what it must have been like being part of a rock and roll version of the F. Scott Fitzgerald crowd in the old days.

However, things were different in the *Let It Be* sessions. Because the studio was downstairs in the basement of the Apple building, the Beatles, et al. more or less merged into the studio from within the building, and the whole atmosphere was a little more relaxed, natural, and conducive to a creative mind-set. One day, George interrupted a meeting between Kass and I with a question concerning a personal business matter. As he apologized for the interruption and quietly made his exit, he stopped and turned in the doorway and asked if I would like to come down to the session. I looked at Kass; he looked at his watch as if to say, "Why don't you go ahead—I've got a lot to do." I think I saw an exchange between them in a glance. I know how Ron Kass thought and did things, and I know he always treated me special. I am sure to this day that he had prearranged the interruption and invitation with all four of the lads, and it was just an experience that he wanted me to have. George was the soft-spoken messenger.

The day I was invited into the *Let It Be* sessions at the Apple studios was second only to the concert on the roof when it comes to experiencing rock and roll genius. I was not only blown away with being one of only two people in the studio (not the lobby, not the control room, but the actual recording studio!) with the four Beatles, but through this experience, I was given the gift of understanding about the very essence of this four-piece band. I never realized how good they were until I sat on the floor, leaning against the wall for hours, and watched them just play their instruments. Everyone was, as we would say in Nashville, a really great picker. I was especially impressed with Ringo. He was the perfect drummer for this band. He laid it right in the pocket and knew how to weave his rhythms in and out, behind, and in support of the raw intricacies of his bandmates. In simplistic terms, he knew how to stay out of the way when it was appropriate, the true sign of a confident, professional drummer. Paul, on the other hand, had the appearance of an eternal force, pushing the band all the time. John's genius

Ken and Ringo chatting at the Apple offices – 3 Savile Row. That's Jackie Lomax's promo picture on the wall. The two ladies are Apple staffers.

would surface, and everyone knew when to fall behind this expression. George, like Ringo, knew how to be supportive of the band as a whole, yet he then would, like everything else in his life, present his unique style gently into the mix of creative musical Liverpuddlian stew. Even when George was blazing forth with electronics seething and screaming, it was always right on—like righteous sonic anger.

The *Let It Be* sessions were an incredible experience for me and the other invited guest into the room—Billy Preston, an old friend and associate who was just as surprised to be there as I was. Billy was a Capitol artist and had a very aggres-

JANUARY 1969

The Beatles' White Album *begins its hold on the #1 spot on* Billboard's *album charts, where it ultimately stays for nine weeks. The single "Hey Jude" drops out of* Billboard's *Top 50 after five months on the charts.*

The Beatles spend the first two weeks of January filming portions of the film Let It Be *at Twickenham Film Studios. George Harrison's* Wonderwall Music *LP enters the* Billboard *charts at #197 on 1/11, eventually reaching #49.*

Filming of Let It Be *continues at Apple Studios on 1/22. Billy Preston joins the sessions; the bulk of what eventually becomes the* Let It Be *album is recorded in the last ten days of the month.*

sive manager who would virtually camp out at my office in the Hollywood Capitol Tower in the days/years before this time. Gene Taft was his name, and Gene was an in-the-trenches, in-your-face manager; nothing was ever good enough for his artist. He even was critical of the way I dressed when we were doing promotions for Billy Preston, to the point of paying to have my suits altered so they would fit better along with the new ties that he had also sponsored to my wardrobe.

Now instead of sitting in my office at Capitol with Gene, Billy and I were sitting in the most famous room in the musical world (which was whatever room the Beatles were recording in at that time). I sat there with fixated eyes and open mouth (I hope I wasn't drooling). I was transfixed by what was going on, totally awed by just how good these guys really were. Off to my right and seated about six feet away, Billy leaned over his keyboards with his hands in his lap and the biggest grin on his face. Every once in a while, he looked over at me with an even bigger smile and a look on his face that said, "Wow, did you just hear that?"

The Beatles would play, they would argue, they would work on something for days only to throw it out. The recording concept was unique and a pleasure to watch unfold. On some days in the control room, the tape was rolling all the time. In the studio, lights were glaring and film cameras were rolling. The walls were stacked almost floor to ceiling with two-inch master tapes. Theoretically, Glyn Johns was engineering, and George Martin was producing, but in reality it looked like their roles were a little less defined. To an observer, they appeared to share the production responsibilities for the project. Interestingly, when the "Get Back" single was released, no producer credit was listed, thus making George Martin's official involvement a little more unclear since he was there and he was their producer.

The Beatles took the approach of recording the songs from beginning to end in the studio. Writing, arranging, rehearsing, recording, and acceptance of final takes was one continuous process. I saw songs grow from inception to the point that one of them would turn around and look in the booth for George's approval and then say, "Let's hear that one." If they liked it, then that was the album master. The idea was to have "live" takes. Looking back, I find it ironic that the album from this session, *Let It Be*, issued more than one year later, featured music that was anything but "live." It wasn't until the Apple-approved *Let it Be...Naked* CD arrived more than thirty years later that the intended "bare bones" approach to the music was finally heard. I will never forget hearing the newly released *Naked* version for the first time. It was a Christmas present from my kids shortly after its release. Decades had passed since I'd sat on the studio floor in the Apple basement hearing the sweet rawness of this fabulous band, and I honestly couldn't believe I had forgotten how incredible the intent and concept of the original recordings had been. I was taken aback by my reaction and surprised to find myself crying. The days and those sounds flooded over me in a dreamy retroactive cacophonic rush as I began remembering what it was all like back then. The jagged expressions that lived in the original sessions came alive, and I was so glad that others would finally get to hear what it was really all about when the greatest rock band of all time was getting back to where they once truly belonged.

Pressing schedules and commitments back in the mother country pulled me off the floor, away from the wall, out the Apple door, down the street, and up to my hotel room to pack. It was cold and gray outside, and the huddled hurrying people in the streets seemed unreal. I felt like I did when I was a kid coming out of a Roy Rogers movie. I always felt like the hero for the first ten minutes or so after walking out of the dark theater into the mundane hometown street. Didn't these people know I had just been in a Beatles session and what a major big deal it was? How can they be concerned with their financial matters, political concerns, and daily routines? I slowly decompressed into their reality, knowing that it was time to "get back" to mine.

It was Tuesday in London and time to go. I walked into my Hollywood office Wednesday morning relaying instructions on the go and piling papers on my secretary's desk. Rocky Catena, Al Coury, Larry Delaney, Roger Karshner, Maurie Lathower, Brown Meggs, Fred Rice, Hal Rothchild, Jack Snyder, Buck Stapleton, Bob York—my executive cohorts in Capitol crime— all dropped in to the office within the first hour, said their quick hellos, asked how it went, and then dumped responsibilities in my lap that had piled up in my absence.

We had a real special group of executives at that time (the late '60s) who genuinely liked each other and liked working with and for each other. As I look back now, I feel fortunate, because not only had I been part of this team and enjoyed these friendships, but also the record business in all its shallow crassness still had a sense of purity about it in those days. I knew I was the hot dog of this group, but they excused me for my youth, tolerated my humor, and respected the giant load of my responsibility by pitching in, covering up, and taking up the slack in my long absences. We were not that well-paid, and for the most part we were there because we were drawn. Back then, you could still believe in something just because you had a feeling and then jump headlong into the project—feet and heart first—with all your energies, money, and time devoted to a new artists' music. Now, the machinery is so big and complicated, the stakes so high, and the overhead so gigantic that it is no longer a business based on creativity and heart but one run by accountants, investors, agencies, powerful management teams, and lawyers. (I am tempted to interject the word ruthless somewhere in the preceding sentences but will leave that up to you.)

In those days, the eighth floor of the Capitol Tower housed the marketing, merchandising, sales, and press and publicity departments as well as my whole operation, which included artist relations, promotion, radio and television services, and internal management of the independent labels. This floor and the twelfth floor, where all the producers and A&R execs lived, were really the throbbing creative centers of this odd round building located at the once-cool Hollywood and Vine intersection of Hollywood, U.S.A.

It was a special time in the recording business because everything was changing—music, mores, and mankind. I often wish we could "get back." For some of us it's hard to just "let it be" in the past.

Message in a Bottle

AUGUST 1995
TWENTY-SIX YEARS LATER

Bodega Bay, California

I found a message in a bottle today! It was almost like rubbing a magic lantern and having a genie actually come out. It is something you read about all your life but happens only in romantic fantasy and the recesses of the unrealized adventure areas of your life. At first, I just stared at it like it would go away because of its tie to unimagined reality. Not only did it stay partially buried in the damp morning sand, but it grew more incredible before my vision the longer I gazed at it.

I bent over to pick it up in a leisurely adventure-story way, letting an ethereal offscreen narrative describe turning seaside pages. It was an absolutely magnificent bottle— thicker than most and a deep clear amber—and smooth, perfect for an extended successful journey to faraway places. The message was in English and clearly visible from the outside—no need to remove the firmly placed cork, no need to break the seal and interrupt its important quest.

The fact that it had been sent on its monthlong journey from a not-too-distant point farther north on the California coast by no means diminished its import or absolute romantic value. Its message possibly fell short of more demanding expectations (it explained the joy that a young couple experienced while draining its contents on a beach blanket in front of a night fire by the ocean). Whoever discovered it was asked to call them after launching the bottle back out to sea so it could continue its odyssey.

I was still entranced with its journey, and because the note was dated, my mind automatically tried to recreate an image of the route it actually traveled in thirty days to traverse a relatively short distance down this rocky, turbulent coast. I could only imagine the storms, the darkness, the cold empty nights, and the curiosity of the sea creatures that examined it on its way. It led me to compare it to the Israelites and their long journey through the wilderness. They too spent a long time traveling a short distance. More than that, I was impressed with the vision of someone that I couldn't see sending me a message from a place I had never been. The message was carried through time and distance via a course I couldn't even comprehend, but the message was in my hand as surely as anything that was ever created.

God sends me "messages in the Bible" much in the same way I was sent this message in a bottle. They come from a time and a place I have never been and speak to me of a time and a place I will someday see. I know that these messages were meant to find their way to me on the beaches of my discontent and confusion. They tell me of the incredible joy to be found in partaking of the contents of the missal that brings it. Even though the preceding may be a shaky analogy in spiritual terms, I find I have just been ministered to by being in daily attendance at my favorite church. A church walled by the wind, carpeted by the sand, and covered with the never-ending expanse of the azure sky and the Son shining down on me. A church that gently reveals the secret shadows, spaces, and deep tide pools of his love and his Word. And just like this message in a bottle, his "message in the Bible" gives me clear instruction as to what I am supposed to do next. Not doing what is written will break the thread of this vessel's purpose and could also keep someone else from ever seeing or sharing in this joy of discovery.

There are other people strolling on the beach this morning, but God calls me to my knees and I obey. He has put some things in my heart that he wants me to ask of him.

Oh Lord, set me out upon the sea of righteousness for your sake; send me with a message to someone in need of your holy Word. Let me wash up on the shore of revelation and let the awesome adventure of a joyful message be clearly visible in me—unchanged by the weather of my trials and disbelief. Put me on the tips of the tides of obedience so that I may ride the crest of salvation into a place you are preparing for me now. Prepare for me a place where I will no longer be adrift on the waves of indifference.

Take me to a place where I will be securely and safely anchored for all eternity in your blessed assurance.

And now in the beckoning sunrise, let me bend down before you and reach into living waters for your "message in the Bible." Set your perfect Word out onto the time-less tides of truth so that it may travel across the sea of forgiveness to these shores of my salvation.

I rise up from the ground, wipe the sand from my knees, and realize I have been weeping and praying out loud. The strollers have stopped and are staring from a safe distance. I turn and walk toward the sun and feel a gentle breeze touch my face and dry my tears. They must surely think I am sad and alone. If they could only experience the joy and peace in my heart—if they could only see who was strolling with me!

Who else but God goes back and forth to heaven? Who else holds the wind in his fists, and wraps up the oceans in his cloak?

PROVERBS 30:4

I'm Only Sleeping

FEBRUARY 1990
FIVE YEARS EARLIER

London, England

A few years ago in London, over lunch, I finally got the opportunity to tell Neil Aspinall what I would have to go through in the U.S. when someone at Apple would let a copy of a new Beatle song slip out of the Apple building. I was also able to explain to him the dilemma I faced when they would plan some new event without filling me in ahead of time. While they had a building full of dedicated employees at 3 Savile Row, I was flying solo as the only Beatles/Apple Records contact in America. This carried on to the point that even after I left Apple and moved to MGM with Ron Kass and Peter Asher, things like the "Paul is Dead" rumor would virtually shut me and my office down for days because of my prior association. I could only imagine what was going down at the Capitol Tower down the street.

I think "World War Three" could have started during the "Paul is Dead" period and no one under thirty would have noticed.

I was fielding calls right and left because since my move from Apple was virtually days old, I was still the go-to-guy as far as most people were concerned. I felt like I was all by myself on the remote American island with no infor-

Ken and Paul—with an apple at an Apple Records function.

mation or warning while my pals, the few remaining Apple execs in London, took the sophisticated approach of dealing with the situation by simply hiding out, shutting off their phones, and locking the doors. This was great for them, but like everyone else, I also could not get through to anyone at Apple UK, plus I didn't have a clue as to what the deal was on the whole issue. Meanwhile, my phones were ringing off the hooks and everyone in the Capitol world and news media world wanted to know what the scoop was. I was supposed to be the "Apple guy," an inside guy, but because I was no longer "in the loop," I didn't know if it was a promo ploy, an aberration, or the truth.

Professionally, I needed to tackle the myriad of tasks at my new job, but I also knew that helping the media solve this "Paul is Dead" mystery was a good move in establishing new kinds of relationships and developing return favors for my new artist roster. The restructuring of MGM was not going to be an easy task, and it was important to build up "capitol" with the people whom I would need to win over to our side in the future as the new product releases hit the street.

Left to my own devices and with definitely no help from my friends on the British Isles, I found a quick solution to the problem. From 1965 to points in time beyond his supposed passing on, I had Paul's signature on various correspondences, documents, autographed items etc. We flew these to a leading criminologist and handwriting analyst in Chicago, and he verified that all the writings and signatures were from the same man—Paul. We were able to document that the dates of these signatures were before, during, and after the rumored death event.

This whole scenario was a little strange in a nice sort of way, because for a few days, it was almost like I was still at Apple, especially because Kass and Asher were with me during this dilemma. We documented, reproduced in leaflet form, and distributed the newly gathered information to all my new staff members at MGM. I instructed them to simply pass on this info in a matter-of-fact manner to the many calls coming into my office. Of course, being a quick learner and following the lead of my English mentors, (or should I say in this case "tormentors"), I locked my office door, ceased taking calls, and moved on from there so I could get back to cleaning up the lion's cage.

I could have killed Paul for not letting me know if he was dead or not!

1969

OCTOBER 1
U.S. release of Abbey Road album.

OCTOBER 6
U.S. release of Beatles' "Something/ Come Together" single.

OCTOBER 12
Disc jockey Russ Gibb of Detroit's WKNR-FM begins broadcasting "clues" detailing Paul McCartney's alleged death.

OCTOBER 14
The Michigan Daily News prints an obituary/review of the Beatles' new Abbey Road album listing even more "clues."

OCTOBER 18
Abbey Road enters the Billboard charts at #178. The album spends 83 weeks in the Top 200, 11 of those at #1. The single "Something" also enters the charts and stays for 16 weeks, one of those in the #1 slot.

OCTOBER 20
U.S. release of John Lennon's "Cold Turkey" single and John and Yoko's Wedding Album.

If I was dead, I'm sure I'd be the last to know.
PAUL MCCARTNEY

Fissures
of Men

OCTOBER 1995
FIVE YEARS LATER

Bodega Bay, California

wish there were a twenty–four hour number you could call to submit a local entry for the most beautiful day on the planet. Today was such a day at Bodega Bay, and I was completely overwhelmed by the fact that God Almighty, Creator of all things above and below, of everything and anything that ever has been or ever will be, loves me so much that he has brought me to these iridescent shores.

It is late October, and everything right seems to happen to the weather patterns along this special stretch of creation this time of year. The textbook tourists are replaced by the faithful few who come here because they have to—drawn by the siren call of the wind, the waves, the foghorn, and what they used to refer to in the Gable and Harlow movies as "it."

I drove to the far end of Salmon Creek Beach, which lies immediately above Bodega Head on the coast. I crawled down the craggy cliff to the rocks below and made my way to the million-mile beach that has a wilderness microcosmopolitanality of its own. Time and topography appear elongated here—the beach towels, picnic baskets, sand castle projects, and artist easels have been set up in quarter-mile distances from each other. As you walk along the beach, it is like going from one small private cosmos to another.

This day absolutely sparkled! I could feel God's presence hovering over the whole scene, and I became alive with anticipation. I knew he was about to weave into this stunning tapestry even greater beauty. Like the warm winds of El Niño sweeping in from the heart of the sea, a message was on its way.

All this wonderfulness melted together in such a way that nature couldn't help but overrespond by outdoing every other aspect of itself. The wind was like Caribbean balm, offering forth a temperature so delicate that you almost had to strain to notice it. The sky vibrated into a glimmering liquid indigo blue. The waves arose orchestrated into a symphony of exuberance, momentarily caught in a continuous finale—crashing, foaming, spiraling heavenward, catching the sun off guard, causing everything to become hazy, diffused, and crystalline all at the same time. Each element and color appeared to flow into each other and then brighten at the idea of the unity. All the shades of the rainbow rushed to occupy every object simultaneously in escalating geometric intensity. Then, in enamored chorus, they gracefully accepted compromise in a moment of colorful celebration by embracing climactic decrescendo into vibrant pastels. The sand pendulated between white and tannish peach, creating the perfect backdrop to whitecaps fraying into alabaster mint drops atop muted Arctic blue surf. The breakers in grateful response sprayed heavenward, engulfing the sun in pale purple reflections.

The Maestro above directed my trance away from this Pacific panorama to the empty shore about a half mile down the beach. Something was barely visible in the mist. I knew where I was going next!

A fishing boat had washed up on the beach! It looked almost embarrassed at its current predicament. The situation was hopeless. The longer it lay there like a king in the mud, the deeper it became immersed in the sand. It was the dichotomy of the day— regal in form, anointed of purpose, and useless at best. Upon closer inspection, it appeared that all the inner workings had been stripped, further diminishing any expectation of restoration. The whole scene threw me into reluctant meditation, and I began shorting out—arcing between this current reality and the impressions born into my very being by the vision of a gentle carpenter walking by the sea.

There was a ghastly hole in the hull. The rocky north coast is known for doing this. As adept as the sailors who commanded this vessel were, they were put to the supreme navigational test when venturing about these shores. The very thing that provided shelter for the bounty that they sought had not been held in high enough esteem to warrant respecting its importance in their lives. They must have violated the No. 1 rule of the north coast and turned their backs on the elements that comprise the sea. Now cast upon the shore of disillusionment, all that they had gathered was lost. They were thrown overboard, no longer in possession of the thing that carried them to their earthly goals. Without their boat, they could no longer fish; they were caught in an abyss, a fissure. No longer fishermen, they became fissure-men!

Jesus could restore their journey.

He could pull them out of this hole.

All they had to do was send out an S.O.S.—

Save Our Souls!

The longer this boat remains grounded, the less chance it has for restoration and being returned to its intended purpose. The more time it spends immersed in the mire, the lower it sinks and the harder it becomes to be saved. So much rot sets in after time that it will take deeper and deeper sanding and scraping. It will require a much longer time in dry dock and need a lot more tender loving care to get it up and out to see again.

Most of all—it will need a new Captain!

And then there are the sailors sailing the seven seas, plying the trade routes of the world. They, too, observe the power of God in action. He calls to the storm winds: the waves rise high. Their ships are tossed to the heavens and sink again to the depths; the sailors cringe in terror. They reel and stagger like drunkards and are at their wit's end. Then they cry to the Lord in their trouble, and he saves them. He calms the storm and stills the waves. What a blessing is that stillness, as he brings them safely into harbor!

PSALM 107:23-30

I've Just Seen a Face

OCTOBER 1968
TWENTY-SEVEN YEARS EARLIER

Hollywood

think one of the greatest joys I experienced as a result of working for Apple and the Beatles may appear to be the most insignificant. It is somewhat of a personalized version of the very thing I found so attractive about them as a group. That thing was their care and loyalty to their old friends, their background, and a sense of who they really were. I too have some old friends, and when I see them, they help me keep on track by reminding me who I really am by our memories.

During one of George Harrison's visits to L.A., he found himself in Hollywood with an hour or so to kill before he was scheduled to go into the studio. He didn't really have time to go back to where he was staying, and he had just come from a luncheon, so he didn't really feel like going to get something to eat to kill time. Instead, he just decided to drop by the Capitol Tower and hide out in my office. It was safe there because of the downstairs entrance security and the protective attitude of the secretaries stationed outside our doors. My office was large, so I could continue on with my calls and work schedule while he just hung out in an easy chair in the corner at the other end, reading Billboard magazine and making phone calls.

After about a half an hour, I totally forgot about him being in the office. He had become quietly and totally absorbed in his reading and, as usual, I was doing eighty things at once while playing my favorite sport: catch-up ball. All was interrupted when my secretary buzzed me from outside. She said a Mr. Bing Drastrup was in the lobby, and the receptionist wanted to know if it was all right to let him come to the eighth-floor executive offices. I said, "Yes, of course. Send him right up."

Like so many of us, I got my start in the entertainment business as an entertainer. During the early '60s folk craze era, I was in a rather successful southern California folk group called the Town Criers. We were signed to a prestigious Beverly Hills management group called Artists Consultants, who worked with acts like Peter, Paul, and Mary and the Gateway Singers during the folk era. For recording, we were signed to Fred Astaire's hot new AVA Records (Elmer Bernstein's "Walk on the Wild Side," Pete Jolly's "Little Bird" or was it "Yellow Bird"?) and were appearing with everyone from Steve Allen and Mitzi Gaynor to Dick Gregory. We were the headliners of Hal Ziegler's 1961 Hootenanny Tour, which sold out major auditoriums all over the country. When it looked like the Limelighters were going to break up, we were RCA's top contender as their replacement. Fortunately for me, I knew I didn't have the performing talent or technical musical skills to make a living as an entertainer for the rest of my life, so I opted to put my Bachelor of Science degree in marketing to use. In time, I bid adieu to the Town Criers dream and headed for the business side of the music business.

Bing Drastrup had also been a member of the Town Criers and was a good friend. I hadn't seen or heard from him in a long time. I was so excited that he was in the lobby

Ken and George at the Hollywood Playboy Club.

that, without thinking, I told them to send him up. A few minutes later, my secretary brought him into the office, and it was great to see each other. Our mini-reunion consisted of the usual— hugs, how-are-you's, gee-you-look-great's, how's-such-and-such, etc.

All of a sudden, Bing stopped in the middle of our exchange and froze. His eyes got big, his mouth hung open, and he stared over my shoulder. I turned and remembered George sitting in the corner reading his magazine. George smiled, nodded hi to Bing, and went back to reading. I honestly think that neither George nor I thought anything about it at first or realized how stunned my old friend must have been to walk into a room where a Beatle was casually relaxing in an easy chair in the corner. I introduced them, explained to George the relationship, and then as was typical, the stance George took during the remainder of our brief three-way chat was that if Bing was my friend then he was George's friend too. After about fifteen minutes, we all had somewhere to go and walked out together.

I wish Bing could have seen the look on his face when he recognized the face he had just seen when he looked over my shoulder!

People are so in awe of fame. I mean, all you have to do is go on the radio or the television once and if somebody sees you on there and they see you down the street, they act different— they're so impressed by it. People forget how to act normal.

GEORGE HARRISON

The Waves and the Word

MARCH 1994
TWENTY-SIX YEARS LATER

Bodega Bay, California

The Bodega Bay harbor, from a distance, has that beautiful picture-book arch to the shoreline that carves a perfect sweeping inlet for about two or three miles. It is bookended on the southern point by giant postcard ragged rocks with crashing waves and splattered airborne foam, and on the north by a long finger of land that can be seen on most maps of the California shoreline—the famous Bodega Head. There is a narrow inlet at the foot of Bodega Head where the ocean sneaks in to create Bodega Bay. This is where one of California's last few active fishing villages still clings to the edge of the Pacific, still clings to the edge of fading times and customs, still hangs on by a fine fishing line to a time that the longtime locals refuse to accept as a memory.

I walk the beach that transits the land mass and the ocean almost every day. Sometimes the only thing more powerful and resounding than the crashing waves is the awesome roar of God's very Word as it washes over me in truth and revelation. It is by his permission that I walk these incredible shores and by his permission that I am actually allowed to listen to what he has to say. Sometimes I am not sure who is talking to me, but he definitely has a way of letting me know eventually who I have been listening to!

The southern end of this strand of sandy beach lies below the exclusive Bodega Harbor Country Club and the wealthy homes that border the golf course. The fortunate occupants look out at both the ocean and the protected Bodega Bay. It is ironic that although from a distance the shoreline and beach look perfect, there are times that up close, when you really see it for what it is, you find a lot of junk and old clinging, rotting seaweed. I believe God began pointing this out to me so I could see this place much the same as he sees me. It is almost as if the waves bring his words of revelation to the shores of my awareness, and conviction washes up the junk of my life where everyone can see it—where it can no longer be hidden beneath the waterline. If it lies there and stays there too long, it gets even uglier and eventually creates such a stench that no one even wants to be around it. If it is not cleared away, I find I can hardly walk through it—in fact, I find my walk becomes totally unpleasant and ineffective.

Then the high tides come rushing in. The water becomes alive and vibrant and completely overpowering in its vastness and unchanging way. It reaches deep into the sand and recovers all the debris that has accumulated on the beach over a period of time—absolutely and completely washing away any remembrance of ugliness and unsightliness. The waves that wash these things upon the shore of my awareness are the waves of his gentle compassion, waves of warning and revelation of those things that are making me stumble as I try to walk in his way and his Word. These same waves I find myself adrift on when I am out of his will are the same waves of living, rushing water that are always pounding on the shores of my conscious until I am willing to cast off the worldly ropes that tie me to Satan's sinking vessels. It is these waves that I can ride on out to his always waiting and forgiving arms, waves that carry me to his solid anchor and safe harbor. As I look out to the sea now, into the risen Son, whose light dances on the water before me, I behold a crimson tide that washes over me, the beach, and the harbor—covering the pain, fear, doubt, worry, and sin that has slowed me down for so long.

The waves continue pounding, reaching higher and higher onto the shore. When they recede, the beach is washed perfectly clean—not a trace of ugliness is left—it has all been washed out into the sea of forgiveness—no one will ever remember that it was even there.

I walk home in the morning mist, dazed by his presence, a lasting presence that seems to walk on the still waters behind me. Like this beach, I too feel like I have been cleansed by his constant and gentle outstretched hands.

We are pressed on every side by troubles, but not crushed and broken. We are perplexed because we don't know why things happen as they do, but we don't give up and quit. We are hunted down, but God never abandons us. We get knocked down, but we get up again and keep going.

So we do not look at what we can see right now, the troubles all around us, but we look forward to the joys in heaven which we have not yet seen. The troubles will soon be over, but the joys to come will last forever.

2 CORINTHIANS 4:8-9, 18

He Was the Eggman

SEPTEMBER 1969
TWENTY-FIVE YEARS EARLIER

Beverly Hills, California

When Allen Klein made his move to take over Apple, Ron Kass had to go! Klein also knew that this would make the well-documented Klein/McCartney contention even more precarious. Somewhere in his research and planning phase, he had gotten a mistaken and overblown impression of my relationship with Paul. He found out that initially Paul, along with Kass, was the sponsor of my position at Apple. The fact that Ron Kass and Paul McCartney were close, Ron Kass and I were close, and Paul and Ron brought me in—then if a=b and b=c, then a=c! Wrong! I did have a good relationship with Paul but not the kind or one of such depth that would allow me to sway his opinion in a matter such as this.

Once Klein had decided he wanted the Apple in his basket, he put into operation what I am told was his standard modus operandi. Typically, he would tunnel his way into an organization or situation, create mass confusion through his own devices, and then (because he was the inventor of the problem) come forward as the genius with all of the answers—obviously the only person who knew how to solve the problem. Simplistically, this is like secretly setting a

SEPTEMBER 1969

The Beatles' White Album *remains in* Billboard's *Top 100 album chart more than forty weeks after release. Plastic Ono Band performs live at Rock and Roll Revival concert in Toronto.*

Allen Klein negotiates a new royalty rate with EMI/ Capitol for the Beatles product. Plastic Ono Band's "Cold Turkey" recorded.

OCTOBER 1969

U.S. release of the Beatles' Abbey Road.

To [Klein] artists are money. To me, they're more than that.

PAUL MCCARTNEY

building on fire and then becoming a hero for putting out the fire and saving the damsel in distress from the flames!

So according to Klein's plan, Kass was out at Apple, and Klein was in L.A. and on the phone to me. He said he had flown in just to talk to me about the new Apple restructuring and to discuss my recent resignation from the company. Since Klein's takeover of Apple, Ron Kass had become the newly appointed president of MGM Records and had recently offered me a vice presidency of that division. Kass and I knew each other's moves by now, and we were very comfortable working together. He had decided to locate in Manhattan in order to keep his European liaisons more accessible. He would commute to the West Coast offices and movie lot while I would head up the Hollywood complex and commute the other direction, where I would occupy a plush execu-tive corner office at the MGM Building in New York City on a part-time basis. (Growing up in Idaho, we didn't have an indoor bathroom until I was a senior in high school. I found that I adapted to my new life easily though, and insisting on a better suite at the St. James was a lot more fun than hiking one hundred yards down a frozen dirt trail to a frosty outhouse behind the barn. This proves the old adage—you can take the boy out of the country but you can't do it unless you offer him a better suite!)

George offered to sign my copy of the White Album *as a kind gesture for my helping him while he was working on the album. He asked what I wanted him to write on it—actually George was offering to say whatever personal thing I wanted him to say so I could kind of show off how close I was to a Beatle. I bashfully replied, "Oh, I don't know—just say something groovy and sign it with love from George Harrison." Well as you can see, that is just what he did. Next time, I thought, I will be a little less vague. In retrospect, it has made the autograph more meaningful because of the personal humor he interjected into it.*

Of historical interest is the fact that at that time, the MGM roster of English, country, jazz, and pop artists had a serious morale problem. Somewhere deep within the corporate MGM lot, it had been decided that the executive staff from the Beatles' Apple Records could possibly be prestigious enough to keep the singing lion alive in the music business jungle a little while longer. My confused musical and marketing background made me uniquely qualified to communicate with these lost souls. The fact that the company had literally gone through five presidents in little more than one year while producing no successful records rather loudly suggested that a good marketing push might be in order to help solve a "slight" image problem. The label's stable of artists—which included Eric Burden, War, Michael Parks (Then Came Bronson), Tommy Flanders (Blues Project), John Sebastian (Lovin' Spoonful), Tompall and the Glaser Brothers, Hank Williams Jr., Petula Clark, and Bruce Palmer (Buffalo Springfield), to name a few—were starting to feel a bit insecure, and it was beginning to look as if the good ship lollipop had just about had its last lick! So out of London and on the next plane to New York, Peter Asher (A&R) and Mike O'Conner (publishing) jumped into the lion's den with newly appointed president Ron Kass and myself (VP of marketing and artist relations). We were all soon eaten alive by these magnificent movie men....

(I'm not going to tell you exactly how this musical lion "sufferari" adventure turned out, but you may have noticed that there is no longer an MGM records!)

When Klein called, I knew he was making an immediate response to my resignation and that he deemed it necessary to sabotage this appointment before I officially left Apple. I was not friendly to him when he called, but he

was persistent, and executive protocol did dictate a sever-
ance conference even in the madness of this situation and
the associated turbulent times. I agreed to meet him at the
Beverly Hills Hotel for lunch and/or whatever. After all, he
had flown in from London to meet me, and there were transitional matters to discuss. Even this concession made me
feel a bit disloyal to Kass, but I knew how I felt about Klein,
and I knew that Kass knew.

It seems that every action-packed, earthshaking meeting
that had to do with my career and future always took place
at poolside, in the Palm Room, or in the lobby of the Beverly
Hills Hotel! Guess where Klein asked me to meet him? We
met in the lobby of the Beverly Hills Hotel in order to have
lunch in the Palm Room. Afterward, he suggested we could
have drinks poolside to finish our conversations.

At first meeting, I wondered how anyone could be so
singularly unattractive yet pleasant to meet at the same time.
Our self-introductions were cordial, although a bit reserved
and brief on my part. Based on misguided information about
my influence on Paul's thinking, Klein wasted no time in
getting to the point. He was up to full speed before we had
cleared the lobby on the way to the restaurant. He made it
very clear that he wanted me to stay on board. More than
that, he was willing to sweeten the pot more than I could ever
imagine. His opening statement was: "I am not sure what
kind of money you are making, but if you will continue on
as U.S. manager of Apple Records, you now earn three times
as much as you did thirty seconds ago!" (Kass had negotiated
Capitol into paying my salary and benefits, so no one at Apple
knew how much I earned as U.S. manager of Apple Records.
Before Klein had made this offer, I was basking in the warmth
of Kass's generous doubling of my previous salary to come to

MGM.) While I was still recovering from Klein's statement and hanging on for dear life to my loyalties, he added that not only would the Beatles remain my responsibility, but he would give me the Rolling Stones and Donovan responsibilities as an added inducement and a few more bright career feathers in my skullcap!

I had been warned about Allen Klein in more ways than one. I had heard all the horror stories, and even as we sat there, I knew I was living in a newly altered world that was personally and adversely changed by his methods and personal aspirations. I loved working with and for Apple and the Beatles, and I really believed we had a good thing—organization and people-wise. Then along comes this squatty New York accountant who had more bad press preceding him than Der Führer himself. He had individually derailed mine and a lot of other people's worlds by upsetting the Apple cart—and here I was being beguiled! You couldn't help being taken in by this guy. He was charming and disarming in some obtuse off-the-wall way that just didn't fit into all my learned responses. I didn't like anything about him, but I enjoyed listening to him, and I liked what he was saying to me.

Because of his honed persuasiveness and my cultural unpreparedness, it was almost impossible to say no to him. He knew I was a total tennis nut, and as part of his personal endearment plan to me, he had made the mistake of bringing up his tennis game in our conversation earlier in the meeting. What happened next, I admit, is absolutely crazy. To this day, I can't figure out my mind-set or understand my actions. I think too much time in airplanes reading novels may have contributed to my unreal approach to this situation. In complete denial of my arbitrative cowardice, I took what I thought was an adventuresome way out by acting cavalier about the whole thing: I challenged this odd-shaped little man to a tennis match. He looked like he spent all his time sitting at restaurant tables or in meetings in windowless rooms. At that particular time, I was playing every day of my life. This challenge was my way to get even for Kass, maintain all my loyalties, and get out from under Klein's super salesmanship spell. In a manner of veiled sarcasm, I told him I would accept his offer if he could beat me in one set of tennis. I would arrange for us to play at the Bel Air Tennis Club the next day, and if he could beat me, I would be on the plane with him the day after that on my way to London and 3 Savile Row. He agreed! Let the games begin—I couldn't wait! I was going to send him home red-faced and with his tail dragging!

I went to see Kass that night and told him what had transpired. I was honest with Ron and told him how tempted I was—the money and prestige and all. I told him how I was torn between my loyalties to him and doing what was best for me, my family, and my career. I sought his advice as a friend and someone I greatly trusted and admired. Ron totally understood, and I knew that as a friend, he wanted the best for me and would have advised me to stay at Apple if he thought it was the right choice for me to make.

He discussed with me the challenge we would undertake at MGM, my responsibilities, and the unique opportunity I would have in the overall corporate scheme of this very prestigious company. He had very little to say about Klein's proposal to me and simply offered one small piece of wisdom as I walked out the door at his house that night into the sweet bougainvillea-scented Beverly Hills air:

"You lay down with pigs, and you get up dirty!"

I went home that night with those words and all the wisdom they carried with them ringing softly in my ears. (I truly loved Ron Kass and feel I learned more from him and

Stanley Gortikov than anyone else in the record business. His early death probably affected me more than any one of the many associates I have known who have passed on. He always seemed to give me special care from the very first.) After his comment, I knew that even though it was a long shot, what I was risking was absolute personal, and in some ways, moral madness: I might be forced to keep my word and go to work for Klein! The position Klein was offering me may have been great for the moment, but someday it was going to be over with Apple and the Beatles, and then for the rest of my professional career I would be known as one of Klein's guys.

I met Klein on the tennis court the next day prepared to back out of my challenge—then I saw him in his tennis outfit. The age-old question was finally answered: Which came first, the chicken leg or the egg? Answer: Both at the same time. All worry left me as I knew this would be a snap. I could wrap this whole thing up without breaking a sweat!

His form may not have been the greatest, but I had over-looked one thing—this was not really a tennis match; it was a negotiation—and Allen Klein was virtually unbeatable in negotiations! He was not about to lose this one, no matter what form it had taken. His business dictionary had only one word in it—win!

I never played better—but I couldn't get the ball past him! He couldn't have looked worse, yet he couldn't have been more formidable. The ball just kept coming back regardless of how hard I hit it or how far I placed it out of his reach. I thought I had gone to tennis hell—this match was eternal and was never going to end! (For those who don't play tennis, a set consists of a series of games. Whoever wins six games first wins the set. There is one caveat though: you must beat your opponent by two games. Therefore if you get to six games and he has five games, it is necessary to get the game score to seven-to-five in order to win the set. You just keep going until one of you accomplishes that two-game spread.)

I finally beat Allen Klein that day by a set score of fifteen to thirteen! I learned the meaning of tenacity as I looked over that sagging net into a face and will that was set like flint. I saw firsthand what a tough negotiator looked like. That day when I extended my arms into the air to serve the ball, the tennis racket wasn't the only thing that was over my head: I was in over my head!

The whole time we played, he talked. First, he sweet-talked me, complimented me, reviewed his awareness of and respect for my past glories. When that didn't work, he tried to fill me with fear of the future and how this would be the great missed opportunity of my lifetime, how my mind would come back to this point in time someday in the near future as I lay desolate and devastated, wallowing in the sad sewer of my wasted career. He then upped the ante and began appealing to my greed. He took me visually to the mountaintop of fame, let me look over the edge, and like the very devil himself, with spoken hand gestures he presented the world of fame and fortune that would lay at my feet when I joined him and his organization. When all else failed, he virtually threatened me in a myriad of unkind ways.

I beat him and then it was over. It was like it never happened. We said good-bye, shook hands, and that was it. All intensity dissipated when this person and his mission walked off the tennis court. I no longer worked for Apple or the Beatles. Klein's next stop was 1750 North Vine, Hollywood, California—the "E" floor of Capitol Records—where he would seek my replacement. I never saw him or talked to him again.

Harbor Lights

FEBRUARY 1995
TWENTY-SIX YEARS LATER

Bodega Bay, California

Tonight I look out across the waters, and Orion—the Hunter—hangs low over the sea, backlit by a gentle half moon. I am in deep thought and obligated to respond in answer to the many questions that seem to come in the form of attacks as to how I can choose, in my own free will, to live here on the edge—a land of seeming perpetual disaster. I have only one answer, which seems so conclusive and monumental to me: I honestly feel this is where God has placed me for this time and in his purpose! While disaster surrounds me—recent earthquakes, floods, mudslides, and economic devastations—I feel serenely protected by his grace.

I write this at the near end of a particularly disturbing time—the second of the 1995 floods of Northern California. This incredible piece of earthly real estate has been doubly deluged with torrential rains, whipping winds, and continuous disaster, threatening our very existence. There has barely been a break between the bad news. Yet at the same time, our home has been a safe shelter in the very center of this storm. The inconveniences have been uncomfortable, but not of the lasting type—not like so many around us who have suffered incredible losses as lifetimes of effort have washed down the Russian River and out to sea in a matter of hours.

The latest and most destructive storms have seemed almost mean in nature. The onslaught was quick and cruel, almost personal as it tore away years of effort without discussion. It has been so immense and overwhelming that I am surprised by my own nonchalance as it passes before me. I finally realize that even though this is a community that is facing this tragedy together, this event is really between me and my God. Though each of us thinks and acts in terms of the community in which we live, when it really comes down to it, we are left face down in our pillows one to one with our Creator.

Through it all, I had a sense of thankfulness. I was blessed with the realization that I was supposed to react and act in terms of my walk with the Lord. This was more than a communal thing; it was a covenantal thing. Beyond my earthly reactions and obligations, I more importantly had to be in proper relationship with my heavenly Father every minute of this ordeal.

* * * *

Instead of "Why Me Lord?" (thank you Kris Kristofferson), it was more a search for the meaning of this circumstance and what I was to learn from it in my walk with the Lord. I felt as if I had crossed a line or even graduated to a new level of worship with this subtle revelation.

We often get so wrapped up in the overall of a situation that we overlook its real purpose—our singular relational commitment with God, the Father Almighty. What may sound self-centered is really understanding the meaning of the many moments that pass before our spiritual eyes. It all really does come down to us and God. Our judgment doesn't come to us only as a corporate thing, but also as an individual thing. We have our corporate responsibilities, but when we stand before the throne of grace, we face the Almighty alone.

I divinely understood that I was not to complain about my portion in this disaster. I was not to go and murmur in my tent against the Lord. Nor was I to question him or to rail out against my circumstance. Instead, I was to give thanks that I wasn't placed among those more severely damaged. I believe I was spared the extreme, so that as they rallied, I was blessed with the commission to pray for them with equal fervor.

As I find comfort in these thoughts, my eyes refocus out onto the harbor, and I observe the moon shadows as they wash across an inky blue black sea that highlights a lonely fishing boat heading past the breakers and into the safety of home port. I too am constantly setting my course toward the safety of the outstretched arms of a loving Savior who promises me rest—eternal rest. I fish all day amidst the seaweed of my weakness, casting daily into the vastness of his Word. I pray each day that I can sail into the harbor of his heart with a catch of godly wisdom that will fill his holds—after all, he holds on to me every minute and dwells within every breath I take.

My heart is in this harbor, my being, in the shelter of his arms.

I have called you back from the ends of the earth and said that you must serve but me alone, for I have chosen you and will not throw you away. Fear not, for I am with you. Do not be dismayed. I am your God. I will strengthen you; I will help you; I will uphold you with my victorious right hand.

ISAIAH 41:9--10

Deklein of the Roamin' Allen Empire

AUGUST 1973
TWENTY-TWO YEARS EARLIER

Los Angeles

It was the summer of 1973. I had just returned to L.A. from a muggy month in Nashville, Tennessee after completing production on songwriter Rick Cunha's *Cunha Songs*. This was his first album for Atlanta-based GRC Records, and we were fortunate in his debut to generate a semi-crossover pop/country hit entitled "Yo Yo Man." I drove there and back in my new Mercedes 350 SL, deciding it was time I found out for myself about the ribbon of highway that formed the asphalt and cement foundation beneath the tour bus homes of the country artists I had been producing. I also wanted to get my "kicks on Route 66" before Interstate 40 totally obliterated its memory.

It was good to be back in L.A. I always felt more comfortable in the Hollywood Hills than I did in the rolling hills of Tennessee, regardless of how much the country songs that I produced and recorded romanticized about it. (I have never quite determined if this was my way of denying my rural roots or whether it was because a backwoods country boy was trying to go "up town," and "down home" was refusing dual

JULY 1973

George pays taxes in the amount of 1,000,000 pounds to Britain's Inland Revenue for the 1971 Concert for Bangla Desh *concert, album, and film projects.*

citizenship.) I truly liked the sunshine, the food, the people, and the fast life in this rock and roll paradise. Ironically, I was able to pay my way in Hollywood by producing hit country records in Nashville. I guess I was putting to use what I was trying to put aside. As my New York Jewish friends would say, "So, go figure!"

It was a clear, dry, hot, Santa Ana weather day, and George Harrison and I were alone at a house I had rented for him in the hills of Beverly Hills. It was a good time for George because not only did he have the No. 1 album, *Living in the Material World*, on the *Billboard* charts for five weeks this summer, but on this particular day he was also sitting with the No. 1 single "Give Me Love (Give Me Peace on Earth)." Not bad for the Beatle in the shadows for so many years. My wife and Pattie Harrison were shopping, and George and I were in the kitchen. He was cutting up veggies and cooking lunch—intent on the task at hand, being cautious with the carrots. He seemed abnormally absorbed—head down and talking as he worked. He had called me into the kitchen to tell me something. Even though it had been almost four years since I had left Apple Records, our personal relationship was ongoing. Now, because I had been there at the beginning of this unfolding episode, he wanted me to be one of the first to know that they were leaving Allen Klein. Ironically, I was at the house that day when he got the telephone call that it was over.

The four of us had been outside by the pool when the call came in from London. The conversation became extended, so the girls got bored and decided to go shopping, leaving me to tell George that we had been deserted. Their departing message was that George's bad manners were going to cost us money on Rodeo Drive and that we were to fend for ourselves as far as lunch was concerned.

The final decision had just been made to dump Klein as the Beatles' and Apple's business manager. It was particularly appropriate that I should hear it straight from George. He was aware of and sensitive to my feelings of allegiance toward Ron Kass, the man Klein had forced out of the presidency at Apple. He knew that this friendship and loyalty were the reasons I left Apple Records and followed Kass to a very troubled MGM records.

I'll never forget the encapsulated atmosphere of graciousness that surrounded us in the kitchen that day. George had a way of making a setting very serene when he wanted to talk about personal things. It was his unique way of keeping everything in a gentle and kind perspective. I leaned against the cabinets as he stirred the upcoming meal in the frying pan. Without intendment, we began talking quietly about our personal impressions of Allen Klein and about our friend Ron Kass. George typically never had harsh words to say about people,[6] and as traumatic as this event was, he maintained this personal propriety. There were disappointments and serious questions about Klein's handling of matters both financial and career-wise, but the tone of George's musings always stayed inquisitive and not accusative.

Even though what was going down with Klein was incredibly important and disturbing at that time, George's interest and mine soon seemed to tire of deep matters in the darkened kitchen. With the bright California sun streaming in through distant windows, our energies became focused on the food preparation task at hand, and our minds wandered to the cool pool waiting outside. I remember that George was barefooted and had on a shapeless, long sleeve shirt and English jeans. (I always called them English jeans because they never looked like our pants; besides, it seemed like English rock and roll stars, especially the guitar players, always had tiny rear ends and little skinny legs. This always seemed to make their pants look different, regardless of the cut!)

During our conversation, this gentle barefoot Beatle with skinny legs and no rear end proceeded to elaborate on why I should become a vegetarian like he was. He told me one reason was that animals experience fear when they sense that they are going to be killed. This fear is released into their system just prior to death, and this fear is what we eat when we eat meat. This fact and other bits of similar information he presented that day put a different slant on hamburgers for me and made the previously unappetizing

---

6   "He's quite nice really. But there's a part of him that's odd. He operates on the basis of: 'do unto others as they do unto you, except you do it first.' Thing is, they think you are going to do them, even though it never crossed your mind." (George on Allen Klein. From his book, *I Me Mine* (New York: Simon & Schuster, 1980).

Leonard Nimoy (Mr. Spock) took this picture of George and Ken sitting by a stream on a 7,000 acre ranch in the Malibu Mountains. George left a recording session in Hollywood, about an hour's drive away, to attend Ken's affair there.

AUGUST 1973

On the Billboard *singles charts, George's "Give Me Love (Give Me Peace on Earth)" is at #32 spot after 12 weeks. Paul's "Live and Let Die" is #2 after 5 weeks, while another single by Paul, "My Love," sits at #40 after 17 weeks.*

On the Billboard *albums charts, George's* Living in the Material World *is in the #4 spot after 8 weeks, having spent 5 weeks at #1. The Beatles'* 1962–1966 *and* 1967-1970 *albums are at #24 and #21 respectively after 17 weeks. Paul's* Red Rose Speedway *is #19 after 13 weeks, 3 of those at #1.*

Paul, Linda, and Denny Laine fly to Lagos, Nigeria to begin recording the album Band on the Run. *The project is complicated somewhat in that Wings band members Henry McCullough and Denny Seiwell quit the group the previous day.*

rice and veggies concoction on the stove look a lot more approachable. There was no place to sit down in the long, narrow, railroad-style kitchen, so I stood transfixed while he softly explained other more spiritual reasons for his culinary bent.

Soon, the phones started going crazy. It was getting late, and I was becoming late for the studio. I said good-bye into the ear without a phone in it and headed for the flats and an all-night recording session.

That day, George planted the seeds that sent me into ten years of metaphysical studies, seven years of vegetarianism, and five years as a favored chela of an internationally famous guru (no, not Maharishi!).

So what was the end result of this prolonged search for ultimate self-realization? The personal realization of what a waste of time it all was. The good news? It left me with an undeniable desire for the ultimate and complete union with what I could only describe then as a "higher source." Now in retrospect, it seems ironic that this long, blissed-out, socially cool, wheel-spinning process drove me back up the dusty roads from whence I came, back to blessed truth and godly teachings. Like the prodigal son, I made a joyous return to wisdom that was spoon-fed to me like sweet well water at the spiritual bosom of my loving mother. This refreshing resurrection of God's love sent me running back securely into the unfailing arms of Christianity.

Blessing
of the Fleet

APRIL 1994
TWENTY-ONE YEARS LATER

Bodega Bay, California

Every town has its annual event, and Bodega Bay is no exception. Every April (springtime on the edge) this beautiful noncity by the bay celebrates the Fisherman's Festival, or Fish Fest as it is known in localeze.

In addition to the area's resident creative tribe and the traveling artists/ crafts people who set up shop in large parking lots on the bayside, the community also sponsors art shows, wine tastings, fish frys, etc., in order to finance local charities and projects for the upcoming year. Bodega Bay boasts a bustling population of 950 people and expects 20,000 visitors each year for the festival. If you live here, "tucking in" and waiting for this event to pass is the only alternative to joining the festivities. Coast Highway One is a lone two-lane winding road in, out, and through town, so you can imagine what a true traffic nightmare it is like!

The weather this year has surpassed all expectations for even the most optimistic, locals and visitors alike. It has been perpetually sunny, warm, windless, and fogless—like never before. No one can remember a prettier year at the bay.

The first day of the Fest was the coldest, rainiest, wind-iest, and dreariest day I have experienced in twenty years of visiting or living here. It not only wiped out all outdoor festivities, which is 95 percent of the whole deal, but it also sent exhibitors and visitors alike scurrying home for the entire weekend in bitter disappointment, further lessening a chance for financial recovery in case of good weather on Sunday. It looked like our little town was going to have to figure out another way to pay for some very important and caring services this coming year.

Sunday, the second day of the planned festivities, turned out to be one of those sparkling clear, shimmering days you see in the glossy travel magazines. I do believe God had some-thing to do with this weather, because Fish Fest Sunday is the day for the "Blessing of the Fleet." This is not only a beautiful concept but spiritually it is one of the most moving events I have ever experienced. If you identify with the sea and if only by proximity gain a love and respect for the rugged men who sail these rough waters and dig like hardened, seasoned farmers for the crops in the watery ground, then within the simplicity of purpose and godly intent of this event lies a blessing not only for the fleet but for anyone who peers into its unfoldment on the waters out beyond the harbor line.

Fishing boats historically gather outside the "Tides Wharf" and wait to be led out to the open sea for their annual blessing. In order to leave the protection of the inner bay where the waters are still and dockage is calm and safe, the boats must navigate a narrow channel out to the waiting harbor and open sea. They follow a lead boat from where the blessings shall flow unto them. This boat carries the local pastor and priest and sets the course for the faithful to follow. By the time the local fishermen enter the narrow passageway, the lead boat has already assured their safe passage by going first. The fishermen follow the course set for them in nautical obedience, and once out to sea, they gather around the lead vessel and are ministered to by the pastor and the priest. Although there is no customary date for this event, it does have traditional roots in Europe and the Roman Catholic Church. Therefore, it is the priest who bestows the blessing on the fleet by casting holy water toward each of the fishermen's boats as they pass before the lead boat. Once all the boats and fishermen are blessed, the pastor marks this moment by throwing a wreath into the waters below. (Pastor Wright told me he once asked the priest where he got the water and what made it holy. The priest jokingly responded that it is tap water and that he boils the hell out of it!)

Once they have received their blessing, the boats return one by one to their home ports within the bay. The source of their blessing is no longer out in front but watches them from the sea as they proceed under the covering of the word. The lead boat returns last, knowing that the flock has returned safely home. From the romantic vessels, you can hear the fishermen's great shouts of joy as they both celebrate and rest in blessed assurance as they sail homeward under the watchful eyes of the local clergy, their loving Father, and in the warmth of their unshaking faith.

This year as they were going out, I couldn't help but notice that it was a narrow channel they had to go through to get to their promised blessing. I also noticed as I scanned back across the inner bay that relatively few of the total boats anchored in the bay made this journey! As I looked at the narrow channel and the rock walls that confine the passage, I realized that these represent the guidelines that Christ sets out for us in his Word. The walls of this channel represent discipline and conformity to the Word. Without discipline, borders, and boundaries to our movements, we would become like lost sheep. I have found that I experience the greatest freedom in life when I give up control and submit to the Ten Commandments, the Word, the urgings of the Holy Spirit, and when I place my life and the life of my family under the authority and guidance of the local pastor that God Almighty has placed over me. The peace and joy of a free and protected life comes with submitting everything to God in prayer—big and little decisions alike.

On everything of import in my life, I seek out the godly advice of Pastor Wright, who gently presides over the Fisherman's Chapel by the Bay here in Bodega Bay. I know I am not a burden to him because we are acting within the dictates of our covenant. He accepts my walk as his responsibility—as a sheep in his flock; I accept him as my spiritual keeper. I consider it a privilege and pleasure to follow his lead as he shows me where to go through the bringing of inspired Word into my life. As my pastor, he speaks truth into my life, and this truth has indeed set me free! I am so relieved to be out of the disguised prison of self-effort that wore me out as a new-ager. During that ten-year period of pseudospiritual folly, I taught meditation, did crystal healings, made astral projections, and produced tapes in million-dollar studios donated by fellow followers. These tapes were then used all over the world to further the cause of these teachings. I do not glorify this time in my life (Have you ever noticed how similar the words new age and sewage are?), but God is faithful, and he promises that he will turn all things to good that Satan meant for evil. I am now gloriously saved by his grace. I'm thankful that God used that time to educate me, completely equipping me to speak out against the lies of the New Age movement, enabling me to speak head-to-head with anyone about the deception that lies in this slippery path. Importantly, I also came away with discipline. Back then, this discipline was needed for what was called our "practices," but now I apply it to setting aside the early hours for devotions. (I know now why the new-agers call it practices—you never get it right! I don't have to practice to be a Christian—I am one! One time and I had it—and I have it forever—and I don't have to practice!)

Anyway, I am conditioned to rise early and prepare myself for time with God. It is now ingrained in me—(because of so much practice!) to read words of wisdom every morning of my life and to spend time in quiet prayer with him. The walls of the channel represent this kind of discipline to me—they lead me to where I am going. I know I must remain on the path and not stray. Like Paul, I must keep my eyes on the prize—the fulfillment of God's purpose in my life (Philippians 3:14).

This day changes the way everything looks—I can see the Bible in the beach, his Word on the waves, Jesus on the jetty, and the Spirit in the sky. As Christians, we celebrate Sunday as the seventh day of Creation, a day of rest. I'll bet each year on this particular Sunday, God takes His day off and goes to Bodega Bay for the Blessing of the Fleet.

He will keep in perfect peace all those who trust in him, whose thoughts turn often to the Lord! Trust in the Lord God always, for in the Lord Jehovah is your everlasting strength. He humbles the proud and brings the haughty city to the dust; its walls come crashing down. He presents it to the poor and needy for their use. But for good men the path is not uphill and rough! God does not give them a rough and treacherous path, but smoothes the road before them.

ISAIAH 26:3-7

Imagine
There's
No Heaven

1965–1990
SOME YEARS EARLIER

Los Angeles, London

I am constantly asked if I got to know any of the Beatles individually and personally during the years I spent with them. I always respond, "Yes, over time I was fortunate to spend time alone and share a comfortable and personal relationship on some level with each of them, that is to say except for John Lennon."

In the early years, he appeared distant and shy but never difficult in my presence. I look back now at pictures of us taken at the August 1965 press conference when we first met. I remember what an intelligent and relatively pleasant fellow he was then, even though he may not have been as accessible as the other three. By the summer of '68, when Apple was cranking up, I noticed a dramatic change. Yoko was encouraging him into world visionary projects, basically expanding his perception of the powerful dynamics of rock and roll, as well the beneficial use of the influence that his fame offered to the world. One thing didn't change though—John carried his heart on his sleeve, and from that same sleeve there was always a gentle hand extended that willingly and naturally wanted to reach out to everyone around him.

Occasionally I found myself positioned next to Yoko at a meeting or an event. (That's me sitting on the bench with her, Chris O'Dell, and Maureen Starr in the Let It Be film and in photographs of the January 1969 rooftop concert.) While John always conversed normally with me, she figuratively withheld the conversational time of day. She somehow gave the impression that I was just too common, or that she was too intellectual to exchange ideas with just anyone. Whether this observation came out of her reality or my own insecurities was of no import—she was with John, I was with Apple, and my instructions from Capitol were crystal clear: "Keep it together!"

In retrospect, I simply think she may have just had a lot of things on her mind and also these were pretty heady times in which she and John were under a lot of scrutiny and hurtful criticism. To be honest, in matters of "The Ballad of John and Yoko," I can attest to being a total non-authority. In fact, I saw a much more pacific and less-interposing Yoko than portrayed in most things I have read about her and John. In fairness to Yoko, she always treated me courteously and with respect, albeit with subdued enthusiasm. The one thing I can avow for sure is that when she was in the room, she definitely never went unnoticed! She could do more with being quiet than anyone I have ever known!

As the curtain began to close on the '60s, on Apple, and on the Beatles as a working band, John seemed to grow increasingly bitter, angry, and cynical. It was probably more apparent to me because of the length of time between my short visits. At times, it was hard for me to be around him, especially when he and Yoko teamed up on me. I found myself desperately wishing I was back on the banks of the Clearwater River in Idaho whenever they began two-teaming me with their sociopolitical worldviews that I couldn't even begin to comprehend. I would be wondering where I was going to get my Eldorado waxed when I returned to L.A. while they preached about world hunger.

I happen to believe that balance should be one of everyone's great goals in life, but John and I were obviously at opposite ends of the philosophic playing field. Spiritually and politically, we weren't even close enough to muster up the content for a meaningful discussion. I knew about Carnauba (car wax), and they knew about Sai Baba. I thought they needed to lighten up. I know now that I needed to get a clue as to what was going on in the world around me.

Early on in the game of life and especially in the Super Bowl of mind games—the entertainment industry—I decided there were two ways to approach matters: be naive or be a cynic. I chose naiveté because it was a lot more fun—plus you never had to take anything too seriously. Being a cynic was a full-time job, not to mention a downer. What's more, you could never take time off. I avoided conflict at all cost. John, however, wanted confrontation to have its own chapter in the dictionary. When he looked for an apartment, as the joke would have it, he wanted one with a dissenting view.

MIND GAMES

One day in early 1969, John and Yoko called me into their ground-floor office at 3 Savile Row to talk about a record that George had brought to Apple's attention. John wanted it released in the U.S. and wanted me to explain my negative position on the record. Because of his passion for the project, I assumed it was his baby, only to find out later that he was championing the cause of his bandmate. At first learning, I wondered why George wasn't in on this meeting, but looking back, I now realize the deeper content of the day's dialogue was really John's department. He and Yoko sat shoulder to shoulder behind one long desk that dominated the whole end of the room. My chair seemed smaller than most, and I'm sure they had the legs shortened so that their guests (victims) would feel even smaller than they already did in their presence.

The recording in question was "The King of Fuh" by an American singer who called himself "Brute Force." Unfortunately the lyrics, due to creative repositioning as the song unfolded, were so blatantly objectionable by American standards that Capitol Records would not be able to even consider releasing it. I explained that I couldn't release a record in the U.S. on Apple or any other label with that kind of lyric. It would be a "brown paper bag under the counter" type of thing at best. Then they started in on me: "we thought you were one of us, Ken...but it looks like you are just one of the establishment like everyone else, after all...we thought we could trust you of all people to understand the concept behind the whole Apple enterprise...we didn't know you were sent over here from the 'land of the free' to act as Apple's personal tight a – -d censor!!"

Mere words can't explain how intimidating they were. From a cowering position it was hard, but I tried to explain it had nothing to do with me, Stanley Gortikov, Capitol Records, or any of our personal beliefs. It had to do with FCC regulations, other legalities, and the like. I don't think I totally convinced them that I was indeed "one of them." As I look back over this lyric debate, it is easy to see the separate worlds we lived in. It is also evident how times have changed since then. These days, few would even comment on this lyric or the *Two Virgins* album cover—except for some possibly unkind observations about Yoko's derrière.

TELL ME WHAT YOU SEE

I will never forget the first time I saw the picture for the *Two Virgins* album jacket. It was 1968, and London was beautiful that summer. We were ensconced in a private suite in a Hyde Park hotel holding meetings with all four Beatles, Neil Aspinal, Ron Kass, Mal Evans, Peter Asher, Stanley Gortikov, Larry Delaney, and Yoko. I left the meeting for a few minutes of attitude adjustment with Mal and had just returned to take my place on the couch with John and Yoko. Quietly, John leaned over, put his hand on my shoulder, placed a packet of photos on my lap, and asked me to "check 'em out." I pulled a dozen or so eight-by-tens out of the envelope and went into executive shock. "Just keep it together," "The Beatles are 50 percent of Capitol's business," and other Hollywood job-security-related admonitions began ringing loudly in my ears. I became transfixed, staring at an armload of nude pictures of him and Yoko. I thought John was making some kind of perverted sexual move on me involving his mate, and I didn't know how to respond. Following what I thought was his lead was totally out of the question, but being so focused on "keeping it together" made me very sensitive to possibly offending him through rejection, thereby losing my job. The wheels were spinning at warp speed in my head. I suddenly became acutely aware that I was just a simple, inexperienced young man in a strange foreign place. I didn't have a clue as to exactly what the ground rules were in matters such as these. I certainly wasn't equipped to handle it! I guess my reaction was fairly noticeable, because when I looked up in desperation toward Stan Gortikov for help, Paul started laughing and came to my rescue.

It seems that while Mal and I were out of the room, John had brought up the subject of his desired approach for the *Two Virgins* artwork and had shown the nude photographs to everyone in the room. Mal and I had missed this presentation,

If the Beatles or the sixties had a message, it was to learn to swim.

JOHN LENNON

and so I was shown the pictures without any advanced instruction. Paul picked up on my dilemma, and after letting me sweat it out for a little while, he finally decided to interrupt my imagined fall from corporate and mop-top grace and filled me in on what transpired while I was out of the room.

I thanked him later, in private, and I asked him, also in private, what he thought of the nude photos bit. He responded that he was totally with John in the matter. He didn't understand John's thinking but figured John was intellectually ahead of him in this area and that he would just have to catch up. He said he was sure at some point that he would catch up and then he would be in complete agreement with John. (Why haven't I ever had a friend like that?)

DAY TRIPPER

I was always nervous about what John was thinking and whether I was "keeping it together" as far as he was concerned. He used to call me, write me caustic letters, send obscenity-laced transatlantic cables to my office in Hollywood, and constantly badger me on a variety of topics, especially those concerning projects on his beloved Zapple record label. (Zapple was Apple's experimental sound sister label. It only released two albums: John and Yoko's *Unfinished Music No. 2: Life with the Lions* and George Harrison's *Electronic Sounds*.) John would communicate encouragement to me when he wanted something done and relay his devastating disappointment in me when he thought I wasn't performing up to speed on Zapple matters.

One time, a person who resembled my image of a raving lunatic more closely than any person I had ever seen parked himself in the Capitol Records lobby and informed the receptionist that John Lennon had sent him to see me. He said he wasn't leaving until he had a proper audience with me as John had instructed and intended.

By this point in my relationship with the Lennons, nothing phased or surprised me. I knew I would have to give this whole scenario a 50–50 chance of being exactly "as John had intended." I said to send the fellow up to my office, where he uniquely occupied a large easy chair without completely bending at the waist. He had, after much practice I'm sure, accomplished a 45-degree liquid linear approach to being seated. He was more than wild-eyed; he was what we called in Idaho walleyed. He eventually organized his one-man free-for-all into the following pitch:

According to him, John had prepared a list of two hundred names of Southern California musicians, artists, poets, and miscellaneous free spirits. He was in possession of this list, and I was to immediately buy first-class one-way tickets to London for this elect group. It seems that John had advised this abstract ambassador from a real nowhere land that the whole of Southern California was going into the ocean in two days, and he wanted to have this particular group preserved for his personal jam sessions and roundabout intellectual gatherings in the U.K.

Apple

Dear Ken   re. Life with the Lions

We'd like the Zapple label
to be SILVER not white — it's
more subtle! o.k?

Also it _must be out_ sooner
than June 2nd. Yoko and I
hope to be there (N.Y.) MAY 26th.
— don't spread it round (too much)
until you hear from Derek Taylor.

t. MAY 15.12 — U. CAN DO IT!
love
John + Yoko xx.

Apple Corps Ltd., 3 Savile Row, London, W.1. 01-734 8232. Cables Apcore London, W.1.   Director, N. S. Aspinall.

This letter and drawing were mailed directly to Ken at the Capitol/Apple offices in Hollywood, California, the first week in May 1969.

Of special note:

- *The letter is handwritten by John Lennon on original Apple stationery.*

- *It includes a line drawing, self-portrait, by John of Yoko and him.*

- *It is possibly the only personal document written by Lennon concerning his pet project—the Zapple label. (The Zapple series was conceived as a subsidiary of Apple Records which would accommodate spoken word, avant garde and experimental recordings. Zapple's first two releases were George's* Electronic Music *and John and Yoko's* Life With the Lions. *Names like Ken Kessey, Lawrence Ferlinghette, Charles Bukowski, Charles Olsen and Richard Brautigan were also batted about as potential artists for the label.)*

- *Lennon shows in this letter his personal involvement with Zapple and his availability to further the project.*

- *Historically, this letter was written by John Lennon during a time of heightened activity in his life (April 21, 1969 to May 16, 1969). He and Yoko had just formed their Bag Productions (April 21, 1969); had changed his middle name from Winston to Ono in a formal ceremony on the roof of the Apple (April 22, 1969); bought Tittenhurst Park, a mansion in Sunnydale, Ascot, Berkshire (May 4, 1969); and signed a business management contract with Allen Klein, along with Ringo and George—Paul refused (May 8, 1969). John was also applying for a United States visa in preparation for his trip to New York (referenced in this letter) to stage a "bed-in." The visa was rejected on May 16, 1969.*

- *Of special interest is the additional Apple/Zapple historical aspect of his request to change the label color and what could be considered as Lennon shorthand (ron for round, U for you), or simply misspelling.*

The only thing odder than walleyed's presentation was the fact that, until I could unconfirm otherwise, I absolutely had no other option but to entertain the possibility that John was actually behind this. To be honest though, I did have serious doubts about believing that John was behind these instructions. The question in the back of my mind was: Why wasn't I on that list? If California was going into the ocean, why wouldn't he want the guy who was working on his Zapple project saved? I was the one with all the information in my head; I had the artwork for the covers on my desk; I had been in the meetings; I was working on a deadline for him that very day. If I went into the westerly waters, he would have to start all over again with a new boy and lose a lot of time!

Fortunately I was able to track John down while my new "friend" took advantage of the kind attentions of my secretary by enjoying about twenty-three cups of coffee with seven sugars each. He seemed surprisingly undisturbed when I told him that John had never heard of him or his ideas. He wished me a nice day, asked my secretary if she had a paper cup for one more coffee to go, and simply walked out to the elevator and left. At first, I marveled at how good-natured he was about the whole thing. He was so intent of purpose and clear of mission when he walked in. Later on, I decided he had probably forgotten what he came to see me about in the first place. (I also felt a lot better knowing that John hadn't left me off the list.)

I SHOULD HAVE KNOWN BETTER

Not all of my memories of John are of an angry young man. In the fall of '69, the Beatles were riding high on the crest of the phenomenal success of the *Abbey Road* album. I felt as though I knew John well enough by this time and had been through enough with him throughout the years to ask just one fan-type question about one of his more oblique lyrics from that album. He was in a particularly receptive mood one day, so I thought I would ask my first Beatle-trivia question. The reason I was so hesitant was that I had seen how incessant the fans and writers were in asking the same incredibly dumb things over and over again. Even though each of the Beatles usually handled them graciously, I could see it was irritating, and they didn't need the people who worked with them doing the same thing.

Anyway, I saw an opening and, after all, I had been saving up for this: "She's well-acquainted with the touch of the velvet hand like a lizard on a window pane" (from "Happiness is a Warm Gun") What does that mean, anyway?" I asked offhandedly, hoping that a casual approach would better my chances of a comradely type response. He grinned and replied, "Nothin'. I just made it up." Smiling gently, he continued softly, as if confiding a secret with me: "We've learned over the years that if we wanted we could write anything that just felt good or sounded good and it didn't necessarily have to have any particular meaning to us. As odd as it seemed to us, reviewers would take it upon themselves to interject their own meanings on our lyrics. So, why 'strain me brain'? Sometimes we sit and read other people's interpretations of our lyrics and think, 'Hey, that's pretty good.' If we liked it, we would keep our mouths shut and just accept the credit as if it was what we meant all along."

It is unfortunate, but I fear most people never got to see this casual, lightness-of-being aspect of John Lennon. I am personally offended by the disproportionate amount of negative verbiage written about other areas of his brilliant life.

TOMORROW NEVER KNOWS

Years later, I was sitting in a London cafe with former Apple president Ron Kass. We were reminiscing about the Apple days and the four lads. When I mentioned that I felt I had never quite gotten to know John, he seemed very surprised. Kass said that out of the four, it was John who had been the most expressive about liking me. Kass said the reason John was so aggressive was because he felt comfortable being open with me. In his own way, he was letting me know that he trusted me.

Up until Kass's revelation, it would have been easier to imagine there was no heaven than to imagine myself as one of John Lennon's favorites. The funny thing about it was in how I perceived John Lennon's music after that. I became a bigger fan and developed a greater appreciation of his lyrics. Now I actually become uncomfortable listening at times because it all sounds so personal.

I DON'T WANT TO SPOIL THE PARTY

In 1976, I unexpectedly ran into John at Ringo's house in Beverly Hills. I had just finished producing Waylon Jennings' new album *Are You Ready for the Country?* for RCA Records, Nashville. Ringo, who was a big fan of Waylon's, had called and asked for an early listen. When I walked into the living room at Ringo's house, I was surprised to see John slouched moodily on the couch. Knowing what I know now, he must have really liked me that day because he had never been meaner. He was in L.A. for his last recording session for almost four years, playing piano on his composition "Cookin' (In the Kitchen of Love)" for Ringo's Atlantic album *Rotogravure*. No doubt he had dropped in to relax and be alone with his old friend and bandmate. I had unwittingly been cast as an intruder by Ringo's invitation that day. Anyway, I needed a lyric change approval from at least three of the Beatles on a female version of "Hey Jude"—which we retitled "Hey Dude"—that I had cut with Jessi Colter ("I'm not Lisa") for Capitol Records. I had bribed Ringo for his signature with a private, exclusive playback of Waylon's album.

I bribed Paul by sending him a pair of sunglasses from Rodeo Drive that he had seen in a fashion magazine. I took advantage of John's mood and bribed him by leaving Ringo's house.

I never saw him again.

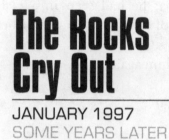

The Rocks Cry Out

JANUARY 1997
SOME YEARS LATER

Bodega Bay, California

It is not all soft windswept moments of paradise wafting across the senses out and up here on the North Coast. Last night, we experienced one of the most dramatic and scary storms that I have ever seen. It thundered full blast out of the Pacific and landed slam bam on the first place in its path—Bodega Bay on the edge.

As the storm battered against the windows and walls of this house I live in, God's Word beat at my heart—the place that he lives in. It was a night of trouble outside and a troubled inside. Scriptures swirled inside my head while his Holy Spirit pressed against the borders of that something inside of me that I can feel but can't quite understand. I prayed and begged for conviction, guidance, and revelation. When he answered me with the truth, I bolted and ran like the wild stallions of my youth—trying to escape back into the distance of the vast Idaho horizons that always beckoned me to go away and beyond in wild expectation of forbidden adventure. I now know from the runnings of my youth that when you chase the wind, it is never at your back. Until Jesus took the reins, I was riding a pale horse into lost oblivion.

It was so easy dealing with life's dilemmas when I didn't have to take my covenant into consideration. God, who is the Way, seems to get in the way when I am trying so hard to do things my way. He stops me in the middle of the muddle and begins to meddle with my motives. He gives me cause to pause and reconsider my course of action. I get so confused that I don't know whether to look up at the shimmering sky or down at my stumbling feet when I am trying to sort things out. I want so much to do things the way he wants me to. But like Paul, I feel like I do the things I am not supposed to do and don't do the things I am supposed to. It seems my heart goes one way and my hands another. My desires and my deals drift daringly downward while his demands drive me in drastically different directions.

O God, listen to me! Hear my prayer!

For wherever I am,

though far away at the ends of the earth,

I will cry to you for help.

When my heart is faint and overwhelmed,

lead me to the mighty, towering Rock of safety.

PSALM 61:1–2

I pray by asking for what I want; he answers with what I need, and I think he has not heard my prayers. In actuality, he has not only listened but has responded with the perfect answer and also with what is absolutely best for me. I ask for wine, and he wants to give me a vineyard; I ask for a pony ride, and he wants to give me a ranch. Unfortunately, my eyes are always on a half-filled glass and a puny pony.

The reason I get confused with the way God works is that I try to understand and obey from my mind. The mind is where Satan has his way with me—no wonder I get bewildered. That is why God asks me to love him with "all my heart"—that is where I am to love him, not from my head. God's ways are so much higher than ours (see Isaiah 55:8–9), no wonder we go crazy trying to figure things out. That is why the whole of the Bible is about faith, believing in God and trusting him. All examples of his relationships with the people in the Bible are based on these precepts, not on how smart people were or how they had God figured out. "Believe on me"; "Trust in me"; "Through faith all things are possible" (see Mark 9:23) are his instructions to us. It is all so very simple—it is just that our human nature makes it so hard for us to be simple!

I love the simple nature of the rugged men who fish in these hard waters for their livelihood. They have an unexplainable relationship with God's provision. Each time these good fishermen leave the safety of the harbor and sail through the narrow, boulder-lined channel in their small fishing boats, I can almost hear the rocks praying out loud for their safe return. Then I think of Peter, also a fisherman, and the time that Jesus told him that he was the rock on which Jesus was going to build the church. Then Peter denied him three times, but upon realizing what he had done, he wept. The rock the church was to be built on cried out with a broken heart.

The rock world cried out to me, and like the prodigal son, I squandered my innocence on the siren's call that enticed me into the pigsties of a decadent lifestyle. But also like the prodigal son, I returned when the rock of salvation cried unto me and offered to cover me with the soft robe of forgiveness.

Like the burnt stones that were used to rebuild the temple, someday our rock-hard hearts will cry no more when we are finally and firmly placed in the wall of his will.

The Bible says that every time someone is saved, the angels in Heaven go crazy with joy, singing, laughter, and dancing (see Luke 15:10). In fact, there is so much joy when a lost soul is saved that I believe the very rocks of life's hard road we have all traveled on in our journey to be with him will all cry out with eternal joy! Thank God for Jesus and the ride he took into the city to meet the destiny of every man. Oh how the rocks around him cried out that day. He rode on the back of an ass down that road knowing he was on his way to having his hands nailed to a waiting cross. Sometimes I act like an ass and just go my own way—afraid to cross the road back to his waiting arms.

I could hear the rocks crying out to me last night as the winds and the sea crashed against them in mighty concert and force. Then in the early morning, the Son shone through the clouds of my confusion, and I found myself sitting on a rock at the water's edge, crying softly. As I prayed for forgiveness, I felt his mercy wash over me like the waves that washed upon the shore before me.

And as I listened carefully,

I could hear

The Rock crying out—

to me.

For I am convinced that nothing can ever separate us from his love. Death can't, and life can't. The angels won't, and all the powers of hell itself cannot keep God's love away. Our fears for today, our worries about tomorrow, or where we are— high above the sky, or in the deepest ocean—nothing will ever be able to separate us from the love of God demonstrated by our Lord Jesus Christ when he died for us.

ROMANS 8:38-39

Across
the Universe

DECEMBER 8, 1980
SEVENTEEN YEARS EARLIER

High Above the Sunset Strip

They say everyone remembers where they were on the days John Kennedy and John Lennon died. As clichéd as this statement may be by now, it definitely is true of me.

I had sold the old Lash Larue estate up in Laurel Canyon that had been my home, hide out, and entertainment center for almost ten years. My career as a record producer had lost its focus and impetus, unfortunately for me, all at the same time. As I drove away from that house for the last time as a resident, it felt like everything was crashing down behind me, like burning buildings eerily reflected in the reluctant rear-view mirror of my maddened Mercedes. I, thus equipped and thus stripped, came rip-roaring out of the canyon of laurels and onto the edge of the cliffs that hovered high above the Sunset Strip. Dumping my antiques, beard, and the cowboy crazies that I clowned around with in the desperate dirt of that ridiculous rodeo that I once called my life, I deposited myself dazed and demi-defeated into a rented modern glass castle with white and steel furnishings. The view ranged all the way from Catalina Island to the San Gabriel Mountains and all of the L.A. enclaves in between. From this perch, I

1980

AUGUST

John Lennon begins recording his first album of new material in six years at New York's Hit Factory.

SEPTEMBER

David Geffen signs John and Yoko to his new Geffen Records label.

OCTOBER

John celebrates his 40th birthday and his son Sean's 5th.

"(Just Like) Starting Over," the new album's first single, is released.

NOVEMBER

The album is titled Double Fantasy *and is released on this date.*

DECEMBER

Double Fantasy enters Billboard *charts hitting #1 in three weeks. It remains #1 for eight weeks, stays on the charts for 74 weeks, and receives a Grammy as "Album of the Year."*

John gives his final interview for Dave Sholin of RKO radio.

could see everywhere and everything—especially that career-wise I was now nearing nowhere with nothing. I didn't know whether to expect the phone to ring with some big new production offer or whether any minute I was going to hear a big flushing sound as it all went down the toilet.

The house belonged to Donald Byrd, the famous jazz musician and lecturer. One of the great features for me, as a producer, was that he had built an office directly off a control booth that looked out into a big home studio. This meant I could run my Hometown Productions, Inc., from my desk while observing the happenings in the studio through the open control room door. This was going to be especially helpful when I had bands rehearsing for an upcoming project. I could listen and watch out of one ear and eye while doing business on the phone without interfering with the creative process that is so sacred in our business. In this adjoining office were floor-to-ceiling wall cabinets across two complete walls that were designed to store tapes and session supplies. When moving in, I had simply piled all my tapes, files, memorabilia, and personal junk behind the doors of these cabinets. I was thereby able to avoid organizing things by simply not opening the doors and conveniently ignoring the contents therein.

For whatever reason, one day I decided to attack this area. I wanted to start pulling out gold records, pictures, awards, etc., to hang on the remaining office walls. Ironically, the first boxes I pulled out of the shelves were filled with things from my Apple days, things that I had never even bothered to unpack at the Laurel Canyon house. It wasn't long before I was sitting on the floor totally surrounded with John Lennon pictures, letters, and signed recordings. I remember I became softly overwhelmed by some enormity that I couldn't understand as I looked at his face and slipped into a contemplative mixture of awe and dreamlike remembrances of the occasions I was in the same room with him. Memories began cascading and merging until I soon became stoned in a moment of recollective confusion. Something was happening inside me, and I was soon lost in trying to put John Lennon, the Beatles, Apple, Capitol, MGM, Andy Williams, the outlaws, Guru Raj Ananda, Idaho, Hollywood, and the deep meaning of disco into some addled perspective of my current digs and dilemma. From far away, an echoing ringing started in my ears, and it finally came rushing full bore into my consciousness as a reality item known as a phone on the desk a couple of feet away. I shook off a regression knockout punch, reached up from my KO'd position on the floor, and, before the ten-count, was saying hello to someone on the other end. All I got in return for this disturbance was a series of sobbings and mottled verbiage that I couldn't make heads or tails of. About the only thing I could understand was a sniffling, wavering, "I-I-I'll c-c-call you back."

The sound of the phone being rocked into its cradle brought me out of my dream, and I started sorting out my John Lennon stuff from the rest of the Beatles days leftovers. Once again the phone rang. By this time, I was basically back in the real world, and Nick Gilder's second attempt to call me was less emotional. I had just finished producing the "Hot Child in the City" glam rocker's *RockAmerica* album for Casablanca Records. Nick was a total John Lennon fan, which was one of the mutual respect glues that held our producer/artist relationship together. His belief in my abilities as a producer could be my ticket out of Nashville music. My respect for his brilliant talent and uncanny understanding of universal rock themes made us close friends and creative compatriots. He was one of the few artists with whom I wanted to maintain an ongoing, continuing personal relationship.

Anyway, by his second phone call, Nick had gathered himself together enough to tell me that John Lennon had just been shot. I was holding a letter from John in my hand. I looked at the pile scattered around me—John was looking at me from everywhere. Telling Nick I would call him back, I laid down the phone and cried.

The news of John Lennon's death had a strange, unexpected effect on me. I had met John Lennon and had worked for him and his company. I also had been yelled at, criticized, and challenged by him. I had actually been a small part of his existence, especially with the Zapple thing, which he personalized by including me in his quest. Upon his death, I suddenly felt removed from any sense of a personal connection. At that point, I took my proper place in the general public as a shocked mourner. My sense of loss and pain was not that of someone who had known him but that of a minuscule thread in the infinite fabric of mankind. I was simply a member of

'NO COMMENT' — GEORGE MARTIN
UNFINISHED MUSIC NO. 2: LIFE WITH THE LIONS
JOHN LENNON/YOKO ONO   APPLE RECORDS
MADE IN MERRIE ENGLAND, NOV. '68

John sent Ken this, "one of the first" copies of the Life With the Lions *album, but Ken didn't notice that John had signed it. Overrun with thousands of LPs in later years, he began unloading most of them at a used record shop in San Francisco. As the buyer for the store was restacking the piles of records,* Life With the Lions *ended this side up on top of one of the stacks where Ken noticed John's handwritten note for the first time. It was immediately retrieved and Ken returned the twenty-five cents they had paid him for the album.*

a society deeply moved by a tragic loss that was shared and felt by us all. It was no longer personal but universal pain that I suffered. I may have met him when he was alive, but like everyone else, I was never going to hear from him again.

Shortly afterward, I listened to John Lennon/Plastic Ono Band, his first solo album, and I began understanding him for the first time. From that point on, I could hardly listen to the music he had made after the Beatles broke up. It was so personal that I would get embarrassed listening to it. I would almost have to look away, as if I was ashamed for eavesdropping or peeping into his most private feelings. Listen back sometime and see if you have ever known a man who laid himself out so raw and naked before all who would listen, learn, care, or understand. I know now that the reason I couldn't understand John when he was alive is because what he was laying out was so incredibly simple. His fame obliterated his message. It was all so simple that he had a hard time making people understand. The end product many times was his frustration.

There's an old Civil War song that perhaps says it most clearly for us all: "Johnny, we hardly knew ye."

Two things were taken away from all of us when John Lennon died. The first was the dream, the warm hope, that possibly we would all someday see the Beatles reunited and returned to us intact.

Something else happened when John Lennon died, and like the Beatles, the second thing was bigger than we could ever imagine. What happened was we ended up with a hero that we didn't want. We didn't want John Lennon to be our hero. We didn't want him to be a martyr for our cause. We just wanted John Lennon to talk to us through his art and music about what was going on around us.

*"Across the universe—something changed our world—
images of broken light which danced before us like a million eyes—
they called us on and on —across the universe—."*

Now we are left alone in his silence....

The Heart
of the Matter

SEPTEMBER 1996
SIXTEEN YEARS LATER

Bodega Bay, California

Late this afternoon, as I made my way to the beckoning shore, I began offering up my usual complaint to God: "How is it that he demands a relationship with me but it seems like he is never there when I seek him?" I always thought that a relationship consisted of an exchange: I talk—he listens; I ask—he answers; I pray—he responds; I seek—he fulfills; we chat—we share; he guides—I obey; I sin—he speaks to me and corrects me; we are Father and son. That is my interpretation of a relationship—two people exchanging things! In the approaching dusk, everything seemed the same: I was pressing in, reaching out, and as usual he was being silent, not there once again. Then suddenly, he spoke. His are not words in the simple sense and yet they are pure dissertations beyond abstraction. It is "une communication à la efficacité supreme." A complete paragraph and extended dialogue is inserted supernaturally into my mind; a total concept becomes a part of my being. In a twinkling of an eye, I know what I know because it has been made known to me by Him in His way! I stopped still in my tracks as he spoke.

He said, "*We have a relationship in the purest form! You pray, and I do answer prayers—I bless you when you don't deserve it; I punish you when you don't understand. You cry out to me with your problems, and you feel I let you down. You hurt me and disappoint me. You get angry with me, and then I fill you with my love. We are close; we are apart. I question you, and you doubt me. We cling to and love each other to the point of tears. Don't tell me, my child, that we don't have a relationship. We are family in the real sense. We are blood of the blood, and we are bound in an eternal covenant. Like any other child who didn't choose his father, you didn't choose me—I chose you! You may try to leave me, like a runaway leaves home, but you can never be separated from me. I am in you, of you, for you, with you—and because you know my Son, you know me, and we are one. You are my child, the apple of my eye. I knew you, created you, delivered you, and have ordained forever with you. We have the relationship the poets can only try to write about! I have given you a book of this love, and I suggest you go home and read it. Then come before me and tell me we have no relationship! I have made you promises that no man can keep! Read the book and search your heart. Be still, and all your senses will feel our relationship as it embraces you completely and for all time.*"

Without realizing, I once again stare into the darkening waves in disbelief. I am lost and found. I am cold, yet my heart is warm. I cry out, and joy flows in. I laugh, and tears fill my eyes. I swirl on the inner edges of a spiritual whirlwind; his power surrounds me. Then I spin out into my helplessness and fall on my knees, begging for his unending mercy, his unfailing grace, his unconditional love. He remembers his promises and forgets my sin. We talk for a moment about eternity, and the hours fly by, until I stand up and find myself wrapped in the glory of a startling sunset and his loving arms.

I retreat from the shore, stumbling in the sands of time—eyes down, hope up. The waves beat against the beach, and his heart beats inside my chest. Once again I realize that he is the heart of all that matters! And once again I am reminded— it's all about forgiveness. Forgiveness!

What happiness for those whose guilt has been forgiven! What joys when sins are covered over! What relief for those who have confessed their sins and God has cleared their record. There was a time when I wouldn't admit what a sinner I was. But my dishonesty made me miserable and filled my days with frustration. All day and all night your hand was heavy on me. My strength evaporated like water on a sunny day until I finally admitted all my sins to you and stopped trying to hide them. I said to myself, "I will confess them to the Lord." And you forgave me! All my guilt is gone.

PSALM 32:1-5

Homeward

APRIL 1970
TWENTY-SIX YEARS EARLIER

Laurel Canyon

I saw a common thread that ran through the very fiber and being of the Fab Four. It was the first, final, main, remaining, overriding, and indelible impression left with me after first meeting the Beatles on Sunday, August 29, 1965, at the press conference held in Capitol Records' Studio A in Hollywood, California.

I honestly believe that the childlike quality of the Beatles that I alluded to in the chapter "Eight Arms to Hold You" is what the young people, starting with the fans in the Cavern days, sensed from the very beginning. I also believe that this attribute is what eventually attracted the mass affection of young and old followers worldwide. This band had a purity of purpose in their music that has remained unrivaled to this day.

Unfortunately, once they had reached the phenomenon stage, modern mankind, in its predictable nature, had to create a media version of this rock and roll innocence. This version, which only occasionally crossed paths with the truth, had a life of its own.

Once this was done, redone, and overdone, then they had to be undone.

Mass hysteria, mass media, mass marketing, and mass messing around with a magnificent mixture of acumen and mesmerizing musical magic eventually turned it all into one major money machine of mass misery. Unfortunately, at that time, the Beatles ended up with most of the misery—most of the money ended up somewhere else.

What the establishment had built up now had to be dismantled because the Beatles weren't cooperating. They insisted on defining their own parameters—musical and otherwise.

In time, the inevitable industry intervention and inter-jection of its own limitations and frailties into their makeup cut deep into the natural core beauty until nothing was left but a corroded outer shell, a fragile facade erected by everyone except the Beatles. Of course, what was left was unacceptable and simply had to be

torn down,

torn apart,

torn asunder.

There was boyish beauty in this benevolent beast though, and as time progressed, one by one I was also privileged to meet and get to know each of Apple's primary supporting players in this unwritten play. I was surprised to find that they also possessed this kindred inner quality that the Beatles had. "Like unto like," it is often said, and Neil Aspinall, Mal Evans, Ron Kass, Jack Oliver, and Derek Taylor in particular seemed to carry the unusual attribute of being aloof, occasionally a little crusty, yet immediately likable. Each had an acceptable eccentricity that drew people into either being a fan or a friend or both. All were extremely capable of carrying out their given devoir, but above all, and to a man, they were fiercely loyal and dedicated beyond any normal human call to duty. They became inextricably swept up into the task at hand and soon were hanging on for dear life to that little bit of existence they once called lives of their own. I don't know if I was invited inside because I was like them or because I was different. I do know that from the day I walked through the Apple doors at 3 Savile Row, I was aware that in the midst of this musical banquet there were worms gorging themselves on the phenomenal fruit that these dedicated men were frantically trying so hard to preserve.

The eventual browning around the edges and rotting of the corps of the Apple due to repeated exposure and intrusion (the greeds and needs) of the outer world was predictable and unavoidable.

My eternal naiveté and potato-bred simplicity saved me. I looked for and only found their goodness and

1970

JANUARY

Abbey Road *is still at #1 spot in* Billboard *after 13 weeks on the charts.*

Ringo, George, and Paul record "I Me Mine" at EMI studios in London. This is the last new Beatles recording until 1994.

Final overdubs by Ringo, George, and Paul for the "Let It Be" single.

FEBRUARY

Plastic Ono Band's Instant Karma *released. It peaks in* Billboard *at #3 the same week the "Let It Be" single hits #2.*

MARCH

Hey Jude *(Allen Klein era compilation album) enters* Billboard *album chart at #3 and peaks at #2.*

APRIL

McCartney *album released.*

Ringo Starr's Sentimental Journey *album released.*

MAY

Let It Be *album released.*

gentle natures. I found them idealistic and still able to dream, vaguely unaware that they were being pulled deep into an externally induced nightmare. Like the proverbial shot that was heard around the world, the sound of this musical monument breaking apart was deafening. This was the day the music died the second time.

```
WESTERN UNION
TELEX SERVICE

•
CAPITOL HOLSA

APPLE LONDON
Q
APPLE LONDON
27121

1.7.69.

ATTENTION KEN MANSFIELD

CONGRATULATIONS Q TO KENNY BOY ON YOUR NEW FAB GEAR GROOVY
JOB. BEST OF BRITISH LUCK FROM THE BRAMWELL OLIVER COMPLEX
OF COMPANIES INCORPORATING THS FAB FOUR
MARY POPPINS
JAMES, JACKIE, IVEYS, BILLY P.JOCK, GEORGIE, PORGIE, RICHIE,
YONI AND ALL AT APPLE RECORDS INC LTD LSD ECT.

P.Z. WHAT A FAB GEAR TEEN-TYPE PIC IN CASH BOX

APPLE LONDON
27121

+(#
     CAPITOL HOLSA
```

Ken received this telegram (most likely instigated by either Tony Bramwell or Jack Oliver—Apple, London) when Capitol Records announced in the trades that, in addition to the U.S. Manager-Apple Records position, Ken had just been appointed Director of independent labels with similar responsibilities, as with Apple to all of Capitol's independently distributed record companies.

Sending their congratulations via their telegram code names, in addition to Tony Bramwell and Jack Oliver, were: Mary Poppins (Mary Hopkin), James (Taylor), Jackie (Lomax), Iveys (Badfinger), Billy P. (Billy Preston), Yoni (Yoko Ono), and the Fab Four (Jock, Georgie, Porgie, and Richie).

I was only a visitor, and for that I am glad. I am particularly blessed to have been visited by them. I feel fortunate I was able to hop on a plane and take sanity-saving side trips into my other executive responsibilities. This allowed me to perform reality checks between those brief excursions in and out of their world.

I saw what I saw, heard what I heard, felt what I felt, and I may have even forgotten what I don't want to remember. I always felt that they liked me. I do know they trusted me, and in order to dig up dirt or caustic observations about these times and these people, I would either have to become a fiction writer or betray that trust.

I admit that my view of the Beatles and Apple is totally jaded, but I love jade, and fine jade is beautiful and enduring.

I treasure my times in and around the Beatles empire—a mystical place that I or time can never return to. My tour was a mystery to me, and definitely magical.

Only a few of us were there....

It will never happen again......

You can never go back homeward!

Father,
Wherever
You Are

OCTOBER 1993
TWENTY-THREE YEARS LATER

Bodega Bay, California

I love the search, the involvement of trying to place my will into yours. I wish I could reach out to you all the time like I do when I am really hurting and pleading on my knees for your presence within me. In the fleeting moments when everything seems OK, I miss the searing intensity of your all-consuming fire blazing in my face —when conviction is hot on my trail and the heat of the trial burns your purpose into my heart. Like a moth, I want to dive into the flame of your truth, die to myself, and then come alive in the pure light of your everlasting love. I long for that special feeling I get when I lay it all down and recognize you as my source, my provider, my everything. My greatest moments are when I feel something touching that spot I just can't put my finger on— that place where you have your hand on me. It's the place from which I reach out to you when I start spinning out, sinking out of sight, out of your sight, plummeting out of control and uncovered into the mire of my selfishness, my will, and my way.

Oh Father, wherever you are, reach down and hear my
cry. Sometimes I look out across the bay and everything
diffuses into prismatic splendor as the tears of worship
cloud my eyes and run down my face, beneath my collar,
and into my soul. Prayers and Scriptures and plead-
ings and confusion swirl and whirl around me like a
tempest across the waves, and I become lost in you. I am
suspended where there is no space and time, where there
is only the awesome unknown that is you before me.

My eyes focus on an odd spot on the sea just short of
the horizon, a bit off to the left and a glimpse away from
the edge of the sky—a place I have never looked at before.
In meditation, I sink down into the deep blue of the lonely
sea and become immersed in your Word as your promises
flow over me. Peace prevails, and you join me in the depths
and comfort me with your perfection and unconditional
love. Then, like thunder, the sea parts, and like Jonah, I
am tossed out on dry land: you save me; you saved me; you
are my Savior. You provide the fiery light that leads me,
the manna that feeds me, and yet I murmur in my tent of
ingratitude. If only I could realize that the cloud before me
is an Old Testament cloud of protection and guidance; if
only I could stop questioning you and just follow the fire
to the promised land.

Oh Father, wherever you are, I long for that same
place. Like Jacob, I wish you would just wrestle me
to the ground, change my name to Faithful and True,
and change my walk. Give me a noticeable limp and
a clear path. Oh Father, wherever you are, let me
come to you and sit under the shelter of your grace
as your glory blinds me to my desires. Please teach

me about the cross, about what really happened that day. Help me to understand your magnificence and the perfect blend of tragedy and victory that took place on that barren windswept hill. Startle me with the immensity of that moment when it was finished and I became gloriously blessed with eternal salvation. I am tired of running ragged around the edges of the torn curtain. Pull me further, Father —farther up the hill of my predestiny and set me before the triple trees of Golgotha. Let me fall within the gaze of the Man in the middle. Because I believe in him, so deeply, let me hear the sweet sound of his voice, his forgiveness, and the astounding invitation to join him in eternity.

Suddenly the warm waves of your mercy deposit me on the shore of this quiet seaside village. I pick myself up and make my way up the beach toward home.

Am I limping, or is that just my imagination?

For all God's words are right, and everything he does is worthy of our trust. He loves whatever is just and good; the earth is filled with his tender love. He merely spoke, and the heavens were formed, and all the galaxies of stars. He made the oceans, pouring them into his vast reservoirs.

PSALM 33:4-7

Mal

JANUARY 4, 1976
SEVENTEEN YEARS EARLIER

L.A., London, and Beyond

knew I would have to write about Mal Evans in this book because it couldn't be about the Beatles without being about Mal. I truly loved Mal. I had never met anyone like him. We developed a friendship and a deep loyalty that I never expect to experience again with another person. We met, and that was it—pals. I believe that Mal guided me safely down the narrow corridors and tight chambers of that proverbial yellow submarine and guaranteed me smooth sailing with his four captains. His verbalized acceptance, approval, and trust of me was passionately imparted to the Beatles, and this I believe helped give me immediate and confident acceptance on their part. Many times I would test the waters with Mal before approaching one of them on a business matter.

He was the first person I met in the Beatles empire—I was possibly the last friend to talk to him before he was killed.

Mal was a big, lovable, soft-spoken, gentle giant of a man. I'll never forget a time in October 1968 when he and I took Jackie Lomax on a tour of the U.S. to promote the album and a single that George Harrison had produced. (At that time, only the single "Sour Milk Sea" was released.) As it was one of our first Apple releases and one of George's first productions, we knew it was important to do a good job. Mal was the consummate road manager; he treated Jackie with the same respect and care that he afforded the Beatles. The three of us had hung out, partied, and shared a casual relationship until we took Jackie on the road. Then things changed; Jackie was now elevated to star status in Mal's mind, and that was the way he was to be treated while we were on the road. Jackie's every wish and desire was taken care of—no different than if he were John Lennon or George Harrison. Mal expected me to act in the same manner. I set up the promotional itinerary, and Mal set up all the incidentals and preceded Jackie's every move, whether it was walking in front of him down the hall or going curbside at the hotel to make sure the limo was indeed waiting. Jackie was always able to go straight from his room into the waiting car without having to suffer the inconvenience of being a star left waiting in a hotel lobby. As with the Beatles, when Mal was in attendance, he was everywhere at once, taking care of everything.

I remember one night in Cleveland when we spent the evening at a local rock club with the music director, disc jockey, and station manager of the main Top 40 station there. We were sitting at a table along a railing that bordered the walkway through the middle of the club. Our table was in a section that was elevated about a foot and a half higher than the floor of the walkway. Jackie and I were seated opposite each other at the end of the table that butted up to the rail. By facing the rail, we looked straight across the aisle, over the heads of the people seated at the lower tables in the section in front of us, and at the stage. Mal was seated directly next to Jackie (which was behind Jackie when Jackie was facing the aisle and stage). The music director was seated across from

Mal and Ken in a private car on a Philadelphia-to-New York City train.
Photo taken by Jackie Lomax.

Mal and next to me, and the disc jockey was seated next to
Mal. Across the six-man table sat the station manager.

Mal had his back to Jackie and was engaged in deep
conversation with the disc jockey about Jackie's record when
a strange thing happened. Jackie and I were sitting in our
seats, hanging over the railing and watching the activity in
the club while the next act was setting up. Suddenly a scruffy
young guy appears right in Jackie's face and starts picking a
fight with what he probably figured was a skinny little wimp
with long black hair and a sissy-type proper accent and all.
Like radar, Mal sensed something was awry with his artist
in this very noisy club. In one motion, he raised up out of
his chair, turned around, and with the added advantage of
the foot and a half riser, was suddenly hovering over this
obnoxious little twit. I only knew Mal's loving and kind
side, but until this night, I had never seen a scarier look
on a man's face or a man who looked any bigger than Mal

1975

DECEMBER

Release of the last ever Apple single, George Harrison's "This Guitar (Can't Keep from Cryin')." It fails to chart.

did when he unfolded that big body out of his chair and, like a raging blowfish, doubled in size. Simultaneously with his repositioning, Mal let out the loudest roar three inches away from and directly into the twit's face. There was no conversation or male posturing or even face saving. I am sure the twit made a record-breaking situation evaluation, because either he disappeared magically or he immediately made a faster-than-the-speed- of-light exit out of the immediate area. Mal stood transfixed for a few long moments just to make sure no more trouble would enter our space and then quietly sat down and returned to his conversation. What I remember most happened a few seconds later. Mal turned back around to Jackie, softly patted him on the arm, gave him a warm look as if to say, "Everything's OK—Mal's here," and then resumed his conversation once again. When I think of Mal, it is that gentle look I see on his face. Of all the times we shared, I think I have chosen to remember him that way.

The promo tour was a success. The record and Jackie Lomax were not.

Of course George was concerned about the record and if our tour was doing any good. He therefore kept in touch with us all during the trip. He surprised us by picking us up at LAX when we flew in after the tour was over. It was so ordinary. He met us at the gate, and the four of us fell in step, talking nonstop all the way out to the car. Nobody noticed us. We were all tired, but still went to George's rented house that evening and listened to music until late into the night.

* * * *

During the Apple meetings, Mal had rented a room in the hotel next to the suite where we would gather each day. During a break one day, Mal motioned me next door and handed me a big cigarette. It was popular in England at that time to carefully roll the tobacco out of a filter cigarette, leaving the paper and filter intact; chop up some hash; mix it with the tobacco; and then repack it into the paper and filter. I was fairly naive in these matters, but I did take a couple of puffs knowing that it was not a totally ordinary cigarette. I also wanted to be cool with my new mates. (Will high school ever let out?)

I walked back into the most important meeting of my life—and possibly Capitol's history —and immediately started having trouble concentrating as well as becoming incredibly paranoid. You can imagine how I felt with not only the Beatles and Apple executive staff but with Stanley Gortikov, the president of Capitol Industries, looking on. To make matters worse, this is when John Lennon started showing me the nude pictures of him and Yoko. Fortunately, Paul knew what Mal had done. It was kind of an initiation trick on the new guy, and that is why Paul came to my rescue when he did. So even if Gortikov had known the condition I was in and disapproved, it would have been of no matter: the Apple corps would have bailed me out because I was now their guy, and I was so obviously cool! I also knew Mal outside of Apple. I knew Lil, his wife. She and Mal and their kids came to L.A. and stayed at my house after the Beatles broke up. The youngsters were thrilled. I lived alone in a large secluded house in the Hollywood hills with a giant swimming pool. Everything was so California—just like they had seen in the movies. The weather was sunny and incredible all the time, and they looked like prunes at the end of each day from spending so much time in the pool.

Mal and Lil eventually separated, and Mal came to live in L.A. By now, I was in the outlaw mode with Waylon, et. al., and so Mal and I became the Englishman and the cowboy—riding hard herd on the Sunset Strip until the sun came up many mornings.

Mal had a rough time in L.A., and things were not going well for quite a long time. I was sitting home late one afternoon working on my tape deck, editing a sequence for an album I had just produced. The deadline was the next day, but that night was the *Billboard* award show. Jessi Colter was up for "New Country Artist of the Year" based on her hit single I had produced entitled, "I'm Not Lisa." As Jessi's producer, I had been asked to accept for her in the event she won, because she was on the road and couldn't attend.

Final sequences are often hard for producers, and I was deep into my work when suddenly my phone rang. I answered, and it was Mal. I asked him how he was doing, and he started rambling on how well everything

Mal and Ken by the pool at Ken's Hollywood Hills home.

was going. Something seemed funny even though he was professing optimism, and in the middle of his good news, I asked him what was wrong. "Nothing is wrong," he said. "Paul and I just worked out some problems, and he is going to give me credit for some of the things I wrote with him—" I interrupted again, asking him what was wrong. "Nothing," he continued, "and besides that, I am signing a production deal with Atlantic Records, and my book is going great, and because you [Ken] were left out of all the other books, I am making sure you are all over it, and—" I knew Mal too well and too long; somewhere beneath all this good news I sensed something I had never felt with Mal before. Something was horribly wrong.

"Mal—Mal," I said. "Stop and listen to me for a second. Something's wrong, isn't it?" There was silence on his end. "We need to talk, don't we?" I asked. Momentary silence. "Yes," he said softly.

"Mal, I can't meet you now because I have to leave for the awards show in a little while, but can we get together later tonight or first thing tomorrow for lunch?"

"Not tonight," he replied. "How about I'll meet you tomorrow for lunch at Musso & Frank, OK?"

"OK, Mal—I'll see you then."

1976

JANUARY 4

Mal dies.

JANUARY 7

Mal is cremated in Los Angeles.

JANUARY 12

Mal was to deliver manuscript of his book Living the Beatles Legend *to publisher Grosset and Dunlap. The manuscript has never been found.*

Some are dead and some are living—in my life I love[d] you more.

"IN MY LIFE"
LENNON & MCCARTNEY

Claudine Longet (facing camera), Mal, Pattie Harrison (back to camera), unidentified person, Jack Oliver (far right) at Ken's party.

"…and, the new female country artist of the year is—Jessi Colter. Accepting for Jessi is her producer, Ken Mansfield." Those were the words I was hearing, but they were way off in the distance, deep in an echo chamber. I saw the words coming out of Flip Wilson's mouth as if in slow motion, and the trophy in his hand was diffused and without shape. Just prior to the announcement, Diane Bennett, a friend and social columnist for the Hollywood Reporter had just come up to me. Putting her arm around my shoulder, she said, "I am sorry about Mal, Ken." I turned quickly. "What do you mean—about Mal?" "I thought you knew," she said uncomfortably. "He's been shot." Flip was extending the award in my direction, and I was ushered onstage, walking in a half-turned position facing Diane. "Mumble, mumble," and then I was back in the audience and at Diane's side.

"Is he OK?" I asked her, and she told me what she knew. Harry Nilsson filled me in a few days later. He told me that it seems that Mal became increasingly despondent that night and began taking large amounts of drugs which only made matters worse. He was staying with his girlfriend, Fran Hughes, and had taken a gun upstairs and locked himself in the bedroom. She was afraid he was going to do something crazy, so she called the police to protect him from himself.... The street rock 'n roll version of the story was that they shot six warning shots into his head that night to keep him from hurting himself.

There is that part in all of us that wants to make us feel guilty or responsible for the death of someone we are close to. For some reason, I can't pin that dragon on myself, even though I was strategically positioned in this event. I think it is because I loved Mal too much to knowingly do anything to harm him or not to be there if I thought he needed me. I also know in my heart that Mal would never blame me. Those were crazy times, and we were all pretty much missing a couple of bottles each out of our six packs in those days. Time and events seemed to drift in and out of reality at their own given pace. Sometimes we would hop aboard our wild horses and ride like blazing daredevils on the frighteningly fast track we had inherited with the fame of it all. Sometimes our mount would stumble, and we would fall off. It was funny at first, because we were young and invincible. We would just jump up laughing, dust ourselves off, and leap back into the fray full force, unabashed and unblinking. The problem is, the ride kept getting faster, and the destination became more and more obscure.

Sometimes we would fall off and not even know it.

Mal fell when I wasn't looking.

A Child's Prayer

SEPTEMBER 1993
SEVENTEEN YEARS LATER

Bodega Bay, California

Oh Jesus, I wish I could trust you to do the right thing. I wish I could count on you to keep your promises and do all the things you say you will do. I wish I could count on you to answer my prayers, to protect me, to provide for me—always to be aware of me, to try to understand how I feel.

If only you could understand what it is like to be here among men who criticize you, speak out unjustly against you, and actually do harm to you. If only you could know what it feels like to try to be good and then have people virtually crucify you for your beliefs. Oh Jesus, do you have any idea what I am going through? Do you have any idea what it is like to cry out to God at an absolutely critical time in life and feel like he is forsaking you? Do you have any concept what it is like to be rejected for good intentions and have evil people chosen over you? If only you knew what it was like to be in the world and yet feel like you are not really of the world. Oh Jesus, I wish you knew what was going on with me and what lies ahead.

You should write a book—a manual so we would have a list of dos and don'ts and examples of the right and wrong ways to do things. You should put things in the book like warnings, guidelines, directions, and then promise you will do everything you say. To make this thing really incredible, you should just burn this information in our hearts until we can really get it into our heads what you are all about.

Oh Jesus, let the penny drop into my soul—I just want to get it! I just want to be everything you want me to be! Sometimes I just fall to my knees—not to pray, but because I am so overwhelmed by your patience, love, and mercy. I am such a jerk, and you keep right on loving me—steadfast even though I just keep on insisting on being in charge.

Well, it's back to the beach. Somewhere between the bay and the harbor I'll find you, and your Word will wash over me just because I asked you to talk to me. Even though I come to you from far away from your will, your way, and your Word, I know you will bend down and hear my cry; you will hear me and answer me and hold me in your hands. You will lead me safely through the mountains. Because you are my God Almighty, I can lie down beside still waters, for you are with me, around me, in me, and for me. I need you now—I need your guidance and wisdom. Touch me with your gracious love, oh Lord!

The very day I call for help, the tide of battle turns.

PSALM 56:9

The Lord God is my Strength, and he will give me the speed of a deer and bring me safely over the mountains.

HABAKKUK 3:19

While My
Guitars
Gently Sleep

OCTOBER 1968

TWENTY-FIVE YEARS EARLIER

Hollywood Hills

A couple of nights after George had picked up Jackie, Mal, and me at LAX, we were kicking back on the conversation pit-style couch at the house that I had rented for George in Beverly Hills. Jackie was upstairs on the phone, and Mal had crashed out in the back bedroom, totally exhausted from the road and his twenty-four-hour vigil as Jackie's protector. George, Alan Pariser, and I were just lounging around downstairs—not really saying or doing anything. Nothing was planned, and the day's activities were over. We were tired but hadn't totally given up on the night. Amplifiers and electronic equipment dominated the living room since both George and Jackie were occupying the house and were working on a myriad of things related to Jackie's debut album on Apple. George was the producer, and the album would be titled *Is This What You Want?* (There was a time, for a time, when George stored his guitars and things in one of the bedrooms at my house in the Hollywood Hills. I was always a little nervous about the responsi-

Left to right: Ricky Nelson, Kristin Nelson, (Ken), Pattie Harrison and George join Ken to celebrate the launching of his "Hometown Productions Inc."

bility of caring for these valuable items. The added fact that the house had become the first stop and layover for many music people from England prompted me to always keep that bedroom closed off. When the house got full and someone wondered why they were sleeping on the couch, they sometimes asked me who was sleeping in that bedroom. I always replied that Mr. Gretsch and his friends slept there.)

Suddenly the doorbell broke the silence, and because it was his house, George voluntarily and methodically got up to answer the door. It was Jack Casady, from Jefferson Airplane, with his bass in hand. He and George had become acquainted along the way, and through mutual relationships between his Artist Relations Department at RCA and Capitol's Artist Relations Department, Jack had found out where we had placed George for his stay. Jack didn't have a phone number, so he just decided to stop by. After a brief exchange of greetings, Jack joined us on the couches, and also tired from travel, he soon drifted out of the almost nonconversation into the previous quiet. Fifteen minutes had barely elapsed when the doorbell rang again. This time, it was Eric Clapton with travel guitar in hand. Same scenario: hellos—light couch conversation—tiredness sets in—it gets quiet again. Twenty minutes later, the doorbell rings once more, and it's Donovan! I have been around a lot of stars, but this was a little different from my normal evening-at-home-on-the-couch routine. Enter Donovan—same format from door to couch, except Donovan's guitar was acoustic. It took him about ten minutes to attain the previous level of laid-back stupor we all seemed to have gathered together to enjoy that evening. No doorbell this time, but a few minutes later, Jackie sauntered downstairs to join us on the now celebrity-ridden couch. Because he had been on the same whirlwind schedule that day as the rest of us, he immediately went from the hellos into the semi-silence *du jour*.

Rock stars are like hyperactive children in a way—and they can only sit and be quiet for so long. George finally reached behind the couch, pulled his guitar over his head, and placed it onto his lap. He then started quietly noodling on something he had been working on. As attentions and volume increased, he in essence gave us all a nice little twenty-minute performance. As he was winding down, Casady plugged in his bass, gently joined in, and took over center stage (couch) as George faded back into the impromptu audience. Without hesitation or invitation, Jackie eventually joined in a few minutes later and took over from Jack. This thing was now becoming a full-fledged guitar pull.[7]

Clapton plugged in and worked his way into Jackie's set, and soon he was flying solo. It had all been very laid back, but now it was starting to heat up. Pariser and I were sitting right in the middle of this on the couch, and we quietly melted into the fabric and prayed that this thing wouldn't go away.

The last act that night was definitely the headliner. Donovan politely took over and absolutely blew everyone away. His vibrant voice soared softly in that intimate setting; the songs he sang and the unique Celtic/folk/jazz style on the guitar was beautiful beyond description. In the lighthearted portion of his set, he introduced us to part of an unfinished work—a song entitled "I Love Me Pants." He wound down his portion—easing us back into the state that George had "pulled" us out of—with a soft Scottish ballad. Mr. Leitch then quietly set his guitar aside, and we returned to our thoughts.

---

[7] *Nashville Tennessee is famous for its guitar pulls. Here is how it works: Several artists, pickers, and/or songwriters get together in a circle and start passing the guitar around. It usually starts out simple and low-keyed, with each person playing a current work in process or a new song they've just written, etc. When they finish their song, the person next to them "pulls" the guitar out of their hand and plays their current fave.*

This may sound blandly interesting and maybe not too exciting, but something always happens during a "pull." Given the artistic makeup and competitive nature of people in the entertainment business, something deep down inside each person in the "pull" makes them want to outdo the person before them. These gatherings eventually take on a life of their own, and by the time you go around the circle a couple of times, you are witnessing Carnegie Hall/Grammy-Award caliber performances! All the stops are eventually pulled out, and everyone's best material begins pouring forth.

One other magic "pull" night was at my house in Laurel Canyon when four of us witnessed a "pull" that involved David Cassidy (whose musical talent has always been highly underrated) and Roy Orbison. There is something about sitting on the couch in front of the fire three feet from one of the greatest talents of all time while he is belting his heart out on "Cryin'," "Pretty Woman," "Blue Bayou," and the like. It makes today's "Unpluggeds" seem impersonal at best.

My first and still one of my favorite blockbuster "pulls" happened the night I was a guest for dinner at Johnny Cash's house. An after-dinner "pull" developed that included Cash, Waylon Jennings, Jessi Colter, Guy Clark, June Carter, and Rosanne Cash. I have always said that when the cowboys party, they make the rockers look like choir boys with training wheels. This goes double when they start "pulling" the guitar!

It ended as it began. No one said anything before, during, or after this little flurry of musical genius. The thing that was interesting about this event—something I think was brought about by the friendships between the people in the room—was how each person communicated their roots that night through their music. No one played what they were known for but more of what was natural to them—an inside thing that few people ever get to see. Entertainers are not known as great communicators on a one-on-one level, but I think each of these friendships grew deeper that night as they shared themselves through their music and got to know a little more about each other. It was pretty; it was poignant; but most of all, it was personal.

When I drove home that night, I was in a trance. It is said that big things happen in threes. The three most important musical events I have witnessed in my thirty plus years in the music business all involved the Beatles: the casual noon cocktail set that they put on for seven of us at lunch during the Apple meetings, this night at George's house where I was in the audience of two, and unquestionably the event of events in my rock and roll life—the concert on the Apple roof. Although it was their last, in my heart, it will always be their best.

The next day, George and I went to Fred Segals' clothing store to buy jeans.

1968

OCTOBER

"Honey Pie," "Long, Long, Long," "Savoy Shuffle," "I'm So Tired," "The Continuing Story of Bungalow Bill," "Why Don't We Do It in the Road," and "Julia" complete the long series of sessions for The Beatles *(the White Album.)*

George Harrison makes a seven-week trip to U.S.A. with Mal Evans and Apple artist Jackie Lomax. Under George's supervision, Mal, Jackie, and Ken Mansfield travel the country to promote the single "Sour Milk Sea." While in L.A., Jackie records new tracks with George for Jackie's LP.

John and Yoko arrested for possession and for obstructing police in the execution of a search warrant.

NOVEMBER

George makes a brief guest appearance on The Smothers Brothers *CBS television show.*

The Old Man and the Sea

NOVEMBER 1993
TWENTY-FIVE YEARS LATER

Bodega Bay, California

Oh God, I love you. I love the way you fill my thoughts, my very being. I especially treasure the times when you overwhelm me with your very presence.

It amazes me every time I am amazed at how you amaze me—it is amazing!

Today I was blessed with your wonder in the ocean, the sand, the sky, the very temperature that surrounded me. You fill me; you occupy me; you teach me; you heal me and guide me; you speak to me through your very Word.

I saw Peter as I watched the nets from the small fishing boats being emptied at a wharf in Bodega Bay today. How incredible it would be to have been one of those fisherman and have you walk up and ask me to go with you—knowing that we would be speaking the words of eternal salvation into lives for generations to come—to the likes of me—undeserving yet one of those odd souls that are truly longing for that unknown truth that only you can reveal. I wonder if I would have dropped everything and gone with you. I fear that I would cling to the nets that engulf me as they do now. I fear that I would hesitate to make the sacrifice that you require. You ask that we lay down our lives for you, and I am still worried about what I am going to wear tomorrow.

I try to picture my reaction to a gentle Man who would approach me on the shore and ask me to commit my life to him and give up my family and my whole existence as I have known it. Knowing me, I would have been intrigued by your open simplicity and boldness of purpose. I wish I could see your face as they saw it on that day. I wish I could have known you then. I wish you were here with me in that form today. I wish I would only believe you better than I do now!

I had always looked forward to getting older. I imagined the peace and serenity of that age, when everything would be quiet and in order. I just didn't realize things would hurt so much. The only thing that doesn't ache these days in my body is my appendix—which was removed when I was in college.

I know now that I blew it. In my youth, I always operated under the premise that if I was cautious with my finances, relationships, and plans for the future, I would have security; but I would miss all the excitement, travel, and fascinating people. So I gladly traded pensions, homes, and retirement plans for the memories of an incredibly spectacular life that only few can imagine. The only problem is, as I get older, my memory is fading, and I am having a hard time remembering all those good times!

Oh God, I love you. Look at me across this ocean before me and touch me; put your arms around me and draw me into your way and your will and your Word. Oh how I long to swim out to you and drink of your living water—water you can walk on; water I can depend on; the water that will support and cleanse me.

Oh God, I love you!

The Lord of Hosts will spread a wondrous feast for everyone around the world—a delicious feast of good food, with clear, well-aged wine and choice beef. At that time he will remove the cloud of gloom, the pall of death that hangs over the earth; he will swallow up death forever. The Lord God will wipe away all tears and take away forever all insults and mockery against his land and people. The Lord has spoken—he will surely do it!

ISAIAH 25:6-8

Kass: Reinventing the Apple

JANUARY–OCTOBER 1986
SEVEN YEARS EARLIER

Nashville, Tennessee

had not talked to Ron Kass in quite some time when out of the blue and into the gray haze of winter in Nashville, Tennessee, I received a call from him at my new Main Mansfield Associates offices in the United Artists Tower. The newly decorated and furnished suite of corner offices was located on Music Row West in the heart of Music City's Music Row and boasted a daily view of "the boys who make the noise." Sixteenth and Seventeenth Avenues are the famous heart of Nashville's Music Row, and a few years ago, these two streets were honored with new names: Music Row East and Music Row West. In addition, they were made into one-way streets in order to handle the tourist traffic flow their fame was attracting. The suite was designed and furnished in plush Art Deco-Moderne motif with the mandatory Beverly Hills peach-and-green colored furnishings, walls, and carpets. The walls were adorned with Beatles pictures interspersed with signed Leroy Neiman and Michael Young paintings. A bit different from the brown shag carpeted offices that adorned most of Music Row in those days!

It was good to hear from Ron. Even though we didn't talk to each other much those days, we were always in touch and had established a lifetime closeness that automatically erased the sometimes long times between communications. We chatted for quite a while, catching up on what had transpired since our last conversation, and then after Ron had established what I was doing businesswise, he asked if I was open to a new proposition. I definitely replied in the affirmative, because every time Ron Kass had made me a business offer in the past, my quality of life and financial statement greatly improved. I awaited expectantly to hear what he had to say, bearing in mind that Ron always painted on large exotic canvases. Even though I knew all this, I wasn't prepared for what he had in mind.

"If we started up Apple Records again, would you come back as U.S. manager?"

After I picked myself up from my peach-covered floor, I managed to ask him what he was talking about. According to Kass, he had just returned from London, and it seems that over the last few months he had held exploratory conversations with some of the Beatles, Yoko, Derek Taylor, Neil Aspinall, Tony Bramwell, Peter Asher, etc. The concept for reconstructing Apple would be to start up the company as an active label again and to staff it only with the original members so it really would be Apple Records and not just some business venture. (Historical note: Apple never did and had not ceased being. Neil Aspinall still ran it out of offices at 6 Stratton Street in London and spent most of his time in the agonizing defense of its assets and purity. It seems Neil went from listening to screaming teenyboppers to screaming at lawyers, a job that continues to this day.) As a practical matter, there were a lot of potential profits that Apple's status could generate from its catalog through re-issues, repackaging, and release of unreleased masters and projects. However, there was one reality that had to be addressed and overcome and that was the "been there, done that" aspect of the financial contribution that the reemergence would require. Ron said the Beatles and Yoko had no interest in that scenario. But because of the conversational interest he was getting, Ron felt that if we were able to put together the funding for the label, he then had a running chance of putting the whole thing back together. So, what he was asking me was, if he was indeed able to reinvent the Apple, could he have my commitment to return as U.S. manager. He wanted this fact to be part of his presentation. As far as I was concerned, what he was really asking me was, "Did I want to return to the most exciting time of my life? Did I want to rejoin my favorite people in the whole world?" The whole possibility rushed over my imagination like a warm tremor, and I said, "Yes." I jokingly added, "On one condition though—that the U.S. office would be located in Nashville this time instead of L.A." I was getting comfortable in Nashville and didn't really want to go back to la la land. Without skipping a beat, he replied that he thought that would be no problem, so "Are you in?" I calmly said, "Yes," into the receiver to my longtime friend. Inside my very being, "yes" was flashing a million times as if in neon, and I thought I was going to explode with joy. Even if Ron's request was the impossible of impossibles, just being considered as an integral and important part of this great adventure was all the payment I would ever need.

Ironically, I was in the midst of putting together some other deals with a new friend who loved the Beatles and who was an expert at locating large amounts of money for plausible business ventures. This was right up his alley—just what

May 1968

"Who's in the Zoo; Some of the Players."

Ron Kass, 33, American. Division head of Apple Records and the former head of Liberty Records International Division. Immaculately tanned, groomed, and tailored, he moved between continents, setting up record deals with the mobility of the United States Army.

RICHARD DILELLO ON RON KASS IN HIS 1972 BOOK *THE LONGEST COCKTAIL PARTY,* PLAYBOY PRESS

he and I were looking for. Whatever else we were working on ceased, and Kass, he, and I began mammoth teleconferencing. It wasn't long before Ted Solomon, Ron Kass, and I were on a plane to London. I had an old suit in my suitcase that I had bought on Carnaby Street in the '60s. This was the same suit that I wore during other Apple meetings, and I was going to pull it out and wear it symbolically at these new ones. More importantly, in his suitcase, Ted had papers reflecting a ten million dollar commitment from investors if the Apple deal was put together. He had the Apple seed money, Johnny!

Here I was, back on a plane to London for Apple meetings—twenty years later — de-tripper-jà vu all over again, Yogi.

Kass being Kass, he had ensconced us in the private St. James Club just off Bond Street, and like Peter Brown many years before, he had prepared our "shedjule" well in advance. The first day we took it easy, walked familiar streets, stood outside 3 Savile Row on the sidewalk talking for about an hour while looking up at the past and imagining ourselves back inside those windows once again. Kass and I wanted Ted to get an inside feeling of the Apple experience before meeting with Neil. We spent the day retracing steps and events for his education and entertainment.

Kass was acting strangely though. He was constantly excusing himself from our activities and also leaving the table at restaurants for long periods during the whole time we were in London. His demeanor was different from what I remembered, and there was a moodiness that I had never witnessed. I also could not remember him spending that much time in the "john" before. He also was moving funny. When we walked about, we teased him that he was walking around so stiffly that it looked like the laundry had put too much starch in his shorts. He shrugged us off with comments about bad airplane food, jet lag, and his personal apprehension about accomplishing the task at hand. We accepted his explanations but in no way let up chiding him about the starched shorts bit. I knew Ron didn't do drugs, and his long disappearances into the various bathrooms puzzled me.

These musings were swept aside as soon as Tony Bramwell joined us and we began meeting with Neil Aspinall. Tony was the promotion manager for Apple and had committed to the new plan. This was a welcomed job opportunity for him since his career wasn't exactly at its sparkling greatest at this particular time. Tony made fun of my old suit and didn't seem to be as overcome by nostalgia as I had imagined. Ted wanted to buy one just like it, Kass said he wouldn't be caught dead in it, and as expected, Neil didn't even notice. (I eventually passed this suit on to my youngest son when he was living in Italy, and he left it there. I guess some people aren't such big history buffs as I am!)

As Neil, Ron, Tony, and I were sitting in local pubs and, in essence, reconducting a modern version of the original Apple meetings, I sometimes found myself "phasing out." This was quite a trip for me. It was almost like I could close my eyes, block out a couple of erratic decades, and it was as if I had never left. There were some differences however. Neil was now mellowed out, or actually rather worn out, with all the unfun aspects of his current responsibilities in looking after the Apple enterprises. He looked great after recovering from a serious heart attack, and I believe that traumatic event gave Neil the blessed freedom to reevaluate his life's work. He explained how he had established a better job description with the lads, and this enabled him to spend more quality time with his wife, Suzie, and the kids. I always liked him a lot, although to this day I have never been quite sure how he viewed me beyond a warmth and courtesy he always extended, although somewhat guardedly.

The years had changed the other men as well. Tony looked scruffy and worn—even a little down on his luck—but still portrayed that aloof cocky attitude that he felt he deserved when he was on top of the promo world in the old days. Kass was still the consummate class act. As to myself, I am sure if form is to remain true, I probably still came off as the expectant puppy dog looking at the world and all it had to offer as a red rubber ball. Actually, I like being naïve, positive, and expectant; but I admit it sometimes is rather inappropriate.

All the while during these meetings, Ted Solomon was in Piccadilly Circus heaven as he listened and watched history being reviewed and revisited. Most of all, though, I think he was most excited about the possibility of it all being recreated. Neil liked Ted, and this was good. Financing was an absolute cornerstone of this whole discussion.

The meetings went well, although vague, which was necessary at this point. This was merely a fact-finding mission, and everyone left with things to think about and assignments to fulfill before we could proceed further. Since Neil always

Ron Kass and Ken outside Kass's Beverly Hills hotel sometime in the late Sixties.

appeared to me to play his cards very close to the vest, I was not sure where he would land on this issue once it edged closer to reality. The one thing that was for sure was that all the duckies had to be in a proper row before any further meaningful discussions could be had with any of the Beatles or Yoko, who represented John's holdings. It was also mandatory that Neil had to be 100 percent convinced that it was a good idea.

Ron's strangeness evolved into preoccupied remoteness as we began summarizing our duties. We tried to create follow-up schedules before we each made our way "Back to the U.S. of A." After an agreed-upon plan was prepared, Ron returned to California. After a long flight homeward, I said good-bye to Ted at Washington D.C.'s National Airport and carried on to Music City U.S.A. with an armload of assignments to accomplish as my part of the impending proposal. We had established a timetable and would all regroup in about two months in order to continue on to the next step—assuming everything was in order.

I couldn't reach Kass after we returned. He didn't answer or return my phone calls. Even his partner at his movie company couldn't find him. I had his sister's phone number and had conversed with her over the years, but she couldn't help me either. Time was running out on the assignment due dates that each of us had committed to as our individual parts of the preparation needed for the next meeting. Yet Kass had dropped out of sight. Since he was the starting point of our efforts, this made zero sense. It all became clear, however, when his sister called me one day and gave me the phone number where Kass was staying in Arizona with his fiancée, Anne. I called the number and Ron answered the phone. He spoke in a soft, leveled tone as he quietly explained what had transpired since we hugged good-bye in London. Upon returning to L.A., Ron went to see a doctor because he hadn't felt well during the London trip and was, quite honestly, uncomfortable the whole time. The doctor discovered a malignant cancerous tumor in Ron's gut the size of a grapefruit. Ron was given six months to a year to live, and that was it.

Without Ron, there would never be the Apple we had envisioned. For some of us, he was the core, the sweetness, and the heart. It was around him we would all rally. When the news of his fate was made known to all of us, I can't remember even one conversation about continuing on with the whole idea. Ron and I must have imparted the "feel" of the whole thing pretty successfully to Ted when we were "educating" him in London as to the essence of Apple, because Ted never mentioned it either. Still, the three of us became closer friends during this time. Both Ted and I visited Ron in L.A. before he died. Kass looked great and held court in dying as he did in living—in a suite at L'Ermitage Beverly Hills. As always, there were little finger things to eat on porcelain plates and unpronounceable champagne on ice if one preferred.

He died October 17, 1986—eight months after London.

I didn't go to the funeral. I couldn't think of him that way.

I didn't ask God why on this one. I really didn't want to know.

Past Tours, Pastures, and Pastors

1937 AND BEYOND

Bodega Bay, California

I spent so much time on the road over the years that airports and hotel check-in counters became more a part of my life than the corner grocery store. I used to fly more miles than pilots and airline stewardesses were allowed to fly by law. I would get on almost any flight anywhere in the world and the captain would wave hello and the attendants would know what book I had just read. At first, I truly enjoyed this exhilarating release into a fantasy world of famous people, fine hotels, and fancy restaurants. Eventually, it all became such a global blur that I remember one morning I woke up in a beachfront penthouse suite in Honolulu and, without even opening the curtains, started preparing my Kansas City itinerary for that day. I knew something was wrong when I got to the lobby and started wondering where all the palm trees came from!

The blur became an excitement in itself. Things had started moving so quickly that eventually I didn't have to be responsible for recognizing their value. Consequently, I was able to become free from any involvement other than indulgence. It all became like a stretch limo ride in an elongated fast lane.

Now I spend most of my time in Bodega Bay facing the ocean; however, when I turn away from the shore and peer eastward, it looks like home—like Idaho. As I gaze up from the tidal edge to the rolling hills that surround me, I sometimes expect to see the Nez Perce Indian bucks of my youth once again ride up on their beautiful paint horses and surge into the waters behind me in free-spirited joyful emergence as they blend into the elements.

Leaving the sea and my past behind, I make my way up the banks from the shore and get lost in the peaceful pastures that surround the coastline here. My hands drop to my side, and I become suspended somewhere between these coastal meadows and the open fields of my youth. Back then, I couldn't wait to escape from the vastness of the northern Idaho wilderness into the big city—L.A., in particular; Hollywood, in superparticular. Like a cross cuisine chef blending exotic ingredients, from that day on I was wending my way back to a place that incorporated mixed elements of my heritage and the colorations of my quest. I stand now on the California coast, looking up at the hills of home. Past and present merge into who I am now. Where I am is looking at where I was.

While fragmented memories of past tours surge through my mind like a scratchy record on a wobbly turntable, pastures past and present pass before my panning vision until my eyes close and come to rest on the pastors of my life—past and present.

If I had to identify two particular moments in my life that absolutely changed everything, that brought into focus everything I would believe in until I cross over, it would be from two godly actions.

The first brought my salvation; the second brought me blessed assurance!

I remember getting off a plane in Nashville, Tennessee. It was a hot, muggy August morning, and there I stood in my misery with three suitcases and three cardboard boxes. I was broke and broken, heavily in debt, with a career and personal life in the proverbial toilet. I had gone from servants, gardeners, housekeepers, cooks, gofers, summer homes, drivers, Mercedes cars, expensive toys, estates, guest houses, fame, bucks, and glory to this: a lonely airport in Nashville, Tennessee, and not much hope!

When it all came down and fell apart in California, I called Nashville and a couple of friends. I was just looking for a soft place to land. David Frizzell, who was riding the crest of a number one record, "You're the Reason God Made Oklahoma," and Tompall Glaser of the legendary Tompall and the Glaser Brothers, answered the phones. They both said, "Come on ahead. We'll give you a place to stay and a helping hand."

Oh God, I didn't have a clue about your magnificence then, yet you had your hand, heart, and eye on me all the way. You knew what you had in mind for me the whole time. While I was stumbling around in spiritual darkness, you had the light on—a light at the door of hope and your salvation, just waiting for me to come home!

I was so burned out when I got there that I had fully intended to jump broken-boot first into "the wild side of life" the minute I got my Dixie bearings. I didn't really like Nashville that much, but I knew the routines of my past visits, and I was ready to remake my Music City "moves" at an even more maddening level. But before I could get up to speed, I met a wide-eyed, woefully big green-eyed, inside and outside beautiful Southern belle almost within moments of my re-arrival on the Music City U.S.A. scene. She caught me up short and gathered me in for the long run. God used her small hands to pull me in and her little feet to walk with me on my way to eternal salvation.

Actually, I arrived in Nashville on a Sunday morning red-eye and was picked up at the airport by an old friend and outlaw artist, Gail Starr. She deposited me and my stuff at Frizzell's lakeside home where I had mooched my first crash. The next day, Monday morning, I was back at "Hillbilly Hotel," Tompall's studio and office complex. He gave me free office space and immediately put me to work producing some songs for his next album. He knew he had to get what little was left of my mind off what had just happened to me.

By Wednesday we were recording, and that night I took a short dinner break with my engineer, Eric Paul (Willie Nelson, Pam Tillis etc.) at a local watering hole, restaurant, and Music Row hangout called Maude's Courtyard. We weren't there ten minutes when two young ladies walked in, one of whom was about as pretty as was legally allowed. They sat down at the next table. I couldn't stop staring at the prettiest one, eventually to the point of being rude. Knowing how gentlemanly and courteous us L.A. hotshots were, I felt I owed her an explanation (and a chance to get to know me better), so when her girlfriend got up to go to the rest room, I casually and correctly got up and sat down at her table to apologize. Upon introducing myself, she replied that she knew my name, because a few years earlier, she had given L.A. a try and had tried to get an interview with me for a job at my company, Hometown Productions. I told her I had just moved to town and offered her my phone number so she could call me if she ever wanted to go out. She didn't exactly snap up that generous offer, but before I left the table, she did give me her phone number in case I wanted to invite her out to dinner.

I returned to Eric, and for the rest of the meal I didn't know if I was eating grits or Peaches Flambé. I was confused, because the last thing I wanted was a relationship. I didn't really believe in the old adage about getting back up on the horse after you had been bucked off. I had more of a "riding herd" approach to Nashville's young fillies in mind. I might also mention, as my story unfolds, that I was about as close to the last thing on this earth that she was looking for. Technically I was still married, dumped, on the rebound, from Hollywood, busted and visibly careening out of control with my hazard lights blinking brightly in Dixieland. If I were a car, I probably would have been totaled. Put that in a Southern town's personal ad and see how many responses you get!

I waited until Saturday to call her because I was so cool and didn't want her to make the mistake of thinking that I was anxious to see her. I got no answer all weekend and just knew she was out of town with some famous cowboy. I made one last try on Sunday night and she finally answered the phone. Upon subtle questioning on my part, she relayed that she had spent the weekend at her folks' farm in Kentucky, a two and a half hour drive away. Well, so far so good; how would she like to meet me for a drink? She calmly rejected that offer but suggested I take her to dinner instead. That was tough because I had almost no money, but wow—she had the softest, warmest voice on the phone.

We went out the following Monday night, and that was that. We haven't been apart since, and that was in August of 1984. I honestly felt I had waltzed into Tennessee and grabbed the best thing Nashville had ever seen. (The only thing I could see that was wrong with her was that she didn't see anything wrong with me.)

There is no question that we fell in love with each other immediately, although there was a lot of questioning on each other's part as to whether we really wanted to do this. She had prayed for a godly man from the streets who had been around and wouldn't want to go back to the wild side of life. She hadn't expected a street with so many pot holes (pot being the operative word here). She had spent the last year in preparation—in fasting and pressing in to her Lord and Savior Jesus Christ. I had spent the last year watching my life totally unravel and responding by digging deeper into the desperation of my metaphysical and mind-altering practices. One night, I brought all this tie-dyed spiritual baggage into her life. She would pray for me and my plight, and then I would leave her place and escape into marijuana and meditation.

We had one continuous argument: "the Way" and "a way." She said Jesus was "the Way" and I agreed that he was "a way"—one of the many ways up to the mountaintop of spiritual unfoldment. It was so frustrating because I could accept her Jesus as an ascended spiritual master who could lead his believers to Heaven. Why couldn't she accept my guru in like terms and not be so single-minded?

Because this point of disagreement was at the very point of her existence, the difference became too much for her to continue, no matter how much she loved me. In the Bible, it says we are not to become "unequally yoked" (2 Cor. 6:14 KJV). The relationship could not continue. She had to make a choice, and she chose Jesus over me. I couldn't figure it out: I would change gurus for her; why couldn't she at least compromise. We were definitely in love, yet she was willing to make this decision.

The deep love she had for her Lord really spoke to my heart when she chose him over me. I saw faith and belief in real terms, and I was so moved by this Christian love that I knew I had to have some of this. Her choice led me to the most important decision in my life: to accept Jesus Christ as my Lord and Savior and to get a fresh start. A few years later (1991), I produced a Grammy-winning gospel album entitled *Homecoming* by the Gaither Vocal Band. I believe I summarized it quite accurately in my acceptance speech when I thanked God for bringing her to me. I then thanked her for bringing me to him! I still stand in utter amazement that in one minute on my knees, all the sins and horrors of my past were erased and I was new, brand new—as pure, sinless, and unstained as a newborn child. I was free, thank God, I was free at last indeed! My life had been like a rock and roll hotel that I had totally trashed, but when I walked up to check out and pay the bill, the man at the counter said someone had already paid my debt. Furthermore, I was welcome to come back any time because I now had a clean record.

I said earlier that two incidences in my life absolutely changed everything—this was the first one. Like the second one, it didn't have to do with words and preaching; it had to do with sacrifice and actions.

To make a long book shorter, we were married a couple of years later, and after a long search, we finally found a wonderful church home called Bethel Chapel in Nashville. I had never belonged to a church before, but the minute we walked in the door and I heard the first song, I turned to her and said, "This is our church." Since impulsiveness was one of the characteristics she had noticed in me early on in our relationship, she looked at me blankly and said that I didn't even know which person in the room was the pastor, so how could I say such a thing! I said it didn't matter, I just knew this was the place we were to worship together.

We became members, and I was soon under the spiritual authority of my first pastor, Brother Ray McCollum. They say as a baby Christian you start out being fed milk in your teachings, and as you mature in your walk, you will be fed meatier stuff. Well, Brother Ray started me out on bear meat from day one! His teachings didn't leave much doubt as to what a daily Christian walk looked like. He took me straight to the main course and said the dessert had already been prepared and would take care of itself. He filled up our plates and stood over us while we ate, making sure we didn't miss a bite. Like a good shepherd, he truly cared for his flock.

His wisdom in ministering to people in the entertainment industry was only surpassed by his understanding and compassion for the situations we would find ourselves in. While under his teaching, I, to my surprise, was faced with even deeper challenges than those that brought me to Nashville and the Lord. These were devastating situations and circumstances, and he was totally bewildered in trying to figure out God's purpose for my pain. One afternoon, out of frustration and compassion, he had us bow our heads, and he asked God to give him half my load! Now here is a man who believed in prayer and truly believed that God answers prayer! This was not a Hollywood "Hey man I love you—call me if I can help" kind of thing. This was a man of God showing pure Christian love. If he couldn't pray me out of this situation, he was going to jump into the middle of my battle and take half the blows. In the Bible, James tells us that faith without action is not true faith. Before me that day, with his head bowed and tears in his eyes, I saw a man act out his faith. I could go to church every day for ten thousand years and never have a better Bible lesson than I received there on the floor of his office. My wife brought me to the Lord, and on that day, Brother Ray brought me into the Lord's ways. On this, the second most important event in my Christian life, he sealed my walk in the Word with his love, and I knew that day that I could never go back. As the disciple said to Jesus when Jesus asked him if he wanted to leave, I am left with the same question: "Where would I go?"

As supernaturally as God moved me to Nashville, he moved me back to California.

SIDE TWO

I have actually seen Jesus two different times in my life. The first time I saw Jesus was deep in the darkest part of Africa when I was part of a missionary group of Christian musicians and music executives who went to the home of voodooism in central Nigeria. I saw Jesus in the faces of the poverty-stricken and downtrodden Christian believers in this corrupt and faction-torn country. Many of them had walked for days and slept on the ground at night just to hear the words and music we brought from the Bible Belt. As we rode comfortably into their village in our air-conditioned van, they pressed in from all sides, arms in the air, singing and clapping their hands with joy as they welcomed us. I will never forget the smiling faces looking up at us in the dust, and for the first time, I saw Jesus's face in their eyes. They loved us because we loved him. They loved us because we were there to teach them more about him and how to worship him in music.

We had hauled in tons of instruments and equipment all the way from Nashville, Tennessee. We spent the days instructing them in the technical and business aspects of a music ministry and the evenings in sermons and concerts with some of the top names in the Christian music industry. These followers had traveled from all parts of Nigeria as well as neighboring African countries for this event. Textbooks, tapes, sheet music, and even guitar strings were impossible to obtain there, even if they had the finances to procure them. But we taught them how to have a music ministry anyway. Our task was to enable them to return to their areas and carry on with new understandings of reaching people through Christian music.

I will never forget the last night that we were there. Seven thousand young and old Africans were on their feet, hands in the air, tears in their eyes, the music in their ears, God's love in their hearts, and cries of joy on their lips as they lifted up praise in worship at this special time. After the last song in the final concert, everyone left the stage except for the leader of our group. He then motioned for the head of the ministry that hosted our visit to come up on stage, and as seven thousand loving brothers and sisters from this far-off place looked on, our host was informed that we were leaving pianos, sound systems, guitars, basses, horns, carrying cases, music stands, lighting, cables, drum kits, mixing boards, and guitar strings behind. The sound of their joy will ring in my ears forever.

The second time I saw Jesus was in the face of my new pastor when we moved to Bodega Bay. When we left our church in Nashville, the membership was over a thousand. When we walked into the Fisherman's Chapel in Bodega Bay, we were sharing the fold-up chairs with about twenty to thirty people. Presiding over this mini-flock was Pastor Art Wright, a retired Army Chaplain who had served and survived two tours of Vietnam. Pastor Art is a six-foot-five-inch tall, white-haired, and bearded gentle giant of a man who looks like a kindly old sea captain. Jesus became real to me through this man. I could see Jesus in him because he made me realize by his Christlike actions what Jesus must have been like, and I realized then that if Jesus were alive today, I would definitely follow a guy like him. I liked what he said, how he acted, and what he believed in and stood for. I especially liked the fact that my new pastor not only taught me about Jesus and his goodness but that this pastor lived his life like the man he worshiped. As my Southern pastor said: "If you are going to talk the talk, you had better be ready to walk the walk!"

Brother Ray McCollum taught me "where the rubber meets the road" Christianity while Pastor Art Wright taught me "by the Book" Christianity so I could prepare myself for the driver's test.

THE OTHER SIDE

I logged millions of miles on the road in the entertainment business, but the longest distance I have traveled in my life was when I put my knees to the floor. I knew all the shortcuts between distant points in the old days, but as a Christian, I find "the Way" is a long haul straight and narrow with no side streets or easy exits.

If I turn back, the signposts of my past sins await to mislead me.

In prayer I press on, and my new vision reviews the brazen bends in bygone byways. The caustic corners of consequences become the center line down the road of repentance that lovingly leads me out onto his holy highway that I now must travel upon.

It's been a stony path leading me to a soft place.

I am reluctant but determined.

I know someday at this journey's end that he will hold my dirty face in his clean hands and all will be well indeed.

He can already see me coming way off in the distance.

It's all about forgiveness!

I'm on the road again.

For I am convinced that nothing can ever separate us from his love. Death can't, and life can't. The angels won't, and all the powers of hell itself cannot keep God's love away. Our fears for today, our worries about tomorrow, or where we are— high above the sky, or in the deepest ocean—nothing will ever be able to separate us from the love of God demonstrated by our Lord Jesus Christ when he died for us

ROMANS 8:38-39

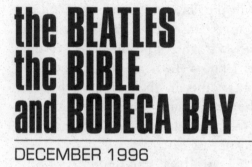

the BEATLES
the BIBLE
and BODEGA BAY

DECEMBER 1996

Bodega Bay, California

Today I found out I have incurable cancer. It is a few days before Christmas, and my reaction is one of peace. I was disappointed to hear this news, but at the same time I had an uncanny sense of relief. Being a Christian really comes in handy in times like these. It was almost as if God was beginning to reveal a new stage in my life. Deep within, where his comforting Holy Spirit dwells, I felt clarity in the mysterious, understanding of the unknown, vision into the unseen. I am in his purpose, and that is all I need to know.

It is quiet on the edge, and the setting sun reveals a majestic sky of deep cerulean blue. I can almost touch the golden linings of the dusk-tinted clouds resting above the sea. The still waters of the inner bay glow softly. Rich purple reflections arise out of the cool, darkened liquid mirror before me.

I fall silent as I look out across Bodega Bay and enjoy my memories of the Beatles and all the people I've known and loved. As I watch the fading sunset, I clutch my Bible in my hands, and I am thankful.

God, I'm no longer scared.

But as for me, my content-ment is not in wealth but in seeing you and knowing all is well between us. And when I awake in Heaven, I will be fully satisfied, for I will see you face to face.

PSALMS 17:15

Blood, Sweet, & Tears

In Dedication

BLOOD
Dale Eugene Mansfield
Kevin Irwin Mansfield
Lisa Dawn Mansfield
Mark Cameron Mansfield
Stuart Alec Mansfield

SWEET
Connie Mansfield

TEARS
Mal Evans
Ron Kass
John Lennon
Linda McCartney
Derek Taylor
Maureen (Starkey) Tigrett

BLOOD, SWEET, & TEARS
Floyd Henry Mansfield
Marian Elizabeth Mansfield
(I can't wait to see you—in the meantime, say hi to Jesus for me.)

Added Infinite Items

Infinite Thanks to

Brent Stoker, a gifted rock and roll era historian, not only for acting as a contributing editor to the Beatles stories but also for helping me to remember where and when I was during these episodic enumerations that seem like wisps on my wavy timeline of existence. Brent contributed unselfishly for over five years without hesitation or reservation, simply for the joy of the journey and the fun of the unfolding friendship.

Bruce Barbour, literary agent extraordinaire, who meticulously guided my long and winding story into major hardcover publication, and to Gwyn Kennedy Snider who then directed the journey into this paperback edition. If talented people are pebbles, then I just sailed into the Strait of Gibraltar. It is great that we all believe in the same Rock.

Bruce Grakal, attorney and longtime friend, who is probably the only person in the world who could have wended our way smoothly through the potentially entangled labyrinth of superstar, mega-industry contracts, permissions, and approvals.

Also to longtime friend Ringo Starr for the initial blessing that made it all much easier.

Nancy Alcorn, founder and president of Mercy Ministries of America (*www.mercyministries.org*). A tithe from the proceeds of this book is dedicated to Mercy Ministries in honor of her vision and unselfish dedication to reclaiming the godly beauty that lies within the hearts and lives of the troubled, precious children that find their way to her open door.

Connie, my wife, my life, my love, my saving grace. And most of all to the Infinite, for the items he has added into my heart and life through *The Living Bible*, the source of the biblical quotations that grace these pages.

I love the Lord because he hears my prayers and answers them.

Because he bends down and listens, I will pray as long as I breathe!

PSALM 116 :1-2

AND IN THE END —

We didn't have time to think things over
We had a lot of fun, we had some tears—
now the highways don't seem so long
After all these years,

"AFTER ALL THESE YEARS"
RICHARD STARKEY & JOHNNY WARMAN
FROM RINGO STARR'S *TIME TAKES TIME* ALBUM
PRIVATE MUSIC 1992

The End

Well, one thing, at least, is good:
It is for a man to eat well,
drink a good glass of wine,
accept his position in life,
and enjoy his work
whatever his job may be,
for however long the Lord may let him live.
And, of course,
it is very good if a man has
received wealth from the Lord,
and the good health to enjoy it.
To enjoy your work and
to accept your lot in life—
that is indeed a gift from God.
The person who does that
will not need to look back
with sorrow on his past,
for God gives him joy.

ECCLESIASTES 5:18–20

Photography
Credits

Song Credits

IN MY LIFE

ACROSS THE UNIVERSE

I AM THE WALRUS

ALL YOU NEED IS LOVE

About
the Author

Ken Mansfield has experienced a life that most people have only read about. He was in the heart and heat of the music industry when it was young and vibrant—back when creativity and passion made the music. A simple young man from the Indian reservation lands in Northern Idaho, Ken found himself propelled into the center of a Rock 'n' Roll whirlwind when as a Capitol Records executive the Beatles asked him to be the US Manager of their Apple Record label as well as acting as their personal liaison between the UK and the US. When the Beatles breakup seemed inevitable, he moved on to become a Vice President at MGM Records and then President of Barnaby Records a CBS label owned by Andy Williams. Wanting to fly even higher and faster, he left the corporate world to set up his own company, Hometown Productions Inc., where he produced famous artists of that era such as Waylon Jennings, Jessi Colter, Don Ho, David Cassidy, Claudine Longet, Nick Gilder, The Flying Burrito Bros. and more.

Ken is the author of six books including the top selling *The Beatles, The Bible and Bodega Bay* (Broadman and Holman) and *The White Book* (Thomas Nelson). Other titles include, *Between Wyomings* (Thomas Nelson), *Stumbling on Open Ground* (Thomas Nelson), *Rock and a Heart Place* (Broadstreet) and *Philco* (Post Hill Press). Ken now lives, loves and writes on the beautiful Florida gulf coast with his wife Connie.